One Lost Sheep

99 Devotionals for Daily Reflections

Brad Simon

One Lost Sheep: 99 Devotionals for Daily Reflections

ISBN: 978-1-954595-18-7

Printed in the USA

Duncanville, Texas

Library of Congress: 2022905333

Published by Sparkle Publishing

www.sparklepublishing.net

Sparkle Publishing

Write. Publish. Sparkle.

Table of Contents

About the Author

William Bradford "Brad" Simon was born in Lockhart, Texas, in 1954. He has been married to his lifelong partner, Nancy Kay, since August 1980. He and Nancy are blessed with three children. Brad and his wife worship and serve at the Lockhart Church of Christ where he serves as an elder.

Brad was baptized in 1964 at the Lockhart Church of Christ. Reflecting on what brought him to baptism at just ten years of age, he recalls a great fear concerning the horrors of hell. Brad believed in God and Jesus, but being born from above and of the Spirit, creating in him a true yearning for God, would not occur until many years later.

Throughout his adolescent years and into his mid-30s, Brad admits to being a part-time Christian, lukewarm at best, full of selfishness and self-righteousness.

God had enough of this behavior and changed his life forever. All praise to Him!

Brad's Testimony

"I know, Lord, that your laws are righteous, and that in faithfulness you have afflicted me."

Psalm 119:75

I remember very clearly the day when my life began to change for the worst, or, at least, I thought it was for the worst. Looking back, I see God's hand in everything He did. He was completely rebuilding me. God was going to change this self-righteous, self-serving man, no matter what it took.

I was 35 years old when I began to question my belief in the Creator, which I kept to myself for a very long time. I was too embarrassed to seek counsel from my parents or go into much detail with my wife. My children were completely unaware. I kept this hidden from the church leadership because, as I mentioned earlier, I was too embarrassed; I was ashamed. How could a person born and raised in the church and a loving Christian household have such thoughts?

Looking back, I see how God worked to make me a new man. I thought of Job and how God allowed Satan to test him, although for a different reason. I was not sure what God was doing in all of this. Through shame and confusion, I was quickly heading into a mental mess. For every positive reason I could think of for the existence of

God, I countered with a negative answer. Frustration began to set in. This went on every day inside my head. I even began to question reality.

After months and years of this torture, I began suffering from depression, the deepest, darkest kind of depression. My mental state was full of misperception with no hope, no future, and no one to rescue me. Thoughts of suicide often entered my mind. I prayed to God with tears but received no answer. My perceived absence of God in my life was horrifying. Had God left me? Did He remove His Holy Spirit from me? I thought of Jesus on the cross in his last few moments of life. He cried to God, "My God, my God, why have You forsaken me?" There was no answer from the Father, only silence. Mentally and emotionally, I was devastated.

This type of suffering went on for 15 years. I would have good days, but mostly terrible days. I would have good nights, but mostly terrible nights. I was scared I would go insane and lose my family and job. Mentally and emotionally, I thought I was at the end. Waking up in the morning only meant another day of mental attacks. I hoped to die during the night. If I didn't wake from sleep, that was okay with me.

I clearly remember the night I contemplated ending my life. It was late, and all was quiet in the house. My wife and children were peacefully at rest. As I was lying there, my next move was to get my pistol. I was minutes from death.

What happened next is hard to describe: God intervened. At that exact moment, the most tranquil feeling I ever experienced came upon me, a poor, pitiful man. I cried. I felt real hope for the very first time in years. I knew this was from God.

I want all who read this to know that without God, I would have never made it. He was with me every step of the way, even though I could not feel Him. There is no other way I could have survived all those years of depression. God was in control when I thought I was by myself. God taught me what being a man of God was supposed to look like. He tore me down and was rebuilding me all this time.

God used one of his servants, Robert Barkley, to comfort me. Through this very special servant of God and dear friend of mine, I was guided in my discovery of real faith. I learned to surrender. I learned that faith *is* surrender. I learned that Jesus is the builder and perfector of my faith, not me. I was beginning to see what birth from the Spirit is all about.

At approximately age 50, with other counseling, I agreed to begin medication for the life-long illness from which I suffer. I began to get educated about clinical depression. I will continue being treated for this disease for the remainder of my life.

God has the desire and power to make you brand new, spiritually, emotionally, and mentally. You are never alone.

If you choose to continue reading this book of devotional thoughts, you will see hints of how God created in me a new man, from selfishness and self-righteousness to humbleness and an ear to really listen to the Father.

Trust God.

All praise to Him!

Acknowledgments

This book of devotional thoughts would not be possible without the support of my wonderful daughter, Ashley. She worked many hours reading, editing, and correcting my grammar and spelling errors (there were many), and filling in my unwritten thoughts. She supported me every step of the way, especially in being so patient with her daddy. Thank you, Ashley!

To my wonderful wife, who always encouraged and supported this effort. I love you!

And to my son, Timothy, who unknowingly inspired many devotional thoughts. I thank you!

Preface

Now that you know about my history and testimony, I want to share an explanation for how this book of devotionals came about. Each and every one of these devotionals stems from a deep-seated desire to better understand my Creator and my relationship to Him. I wanted to delve into the Word and truly study it, not just read it and forget what I had read, as I did before.

Initially, these writings were shared with a few family members. Later, they were passed on to a few church friends, eventually being shared on Facebook occasionally. Finally, I created a group text message that would receive my devotionals regularly (whenever I would come up with a new one), and there would be some discussion back and forth. Their encouragement inspired me to continue this effort.

If asked how I came up with devotionals, or if I noticed a person struggling in the way in which I struggled, I would share my testimony and encourage them to seek help. All of these devotionals have helped me become closer to God and to better understand my relationship to Him. I hope they will help you to do the same.

1 John 1:1

The book of 1 John is a letter written by the apostle John to the believers in Asia or modern-day Turkey. The first letter of three was written between the years of 85 and 95, after Jesus' ascension into Heaven.

> *That which was from the beginning, which we have heard, which we have seen with our eyes, which we have looked at and our hands have touched – this we proclaim concerning the Word of life* (1 John 1:1).

Devotional thought: The apostle John is telling his readers that he interacted with the One who was from the beginning: The King who came to show compassion to the heavy laden, to give peace to the weary, and to save that which was lost. John touched the One who desires to touch our lives. John saw the One that sees our frailties. John heard the One that hears our appeals.

For three years, John witnessed Jesus' walk on Earth. After the resurrection and ascension of Jesus into Heaven, John was convinced he heard, saw, and touched "that which was from the beginning."

Prayer starter: O, God, to have been there to hear, see, and touch that which was from the beginning!

2 Corinthians 1:3-4

The book of 2 Corinthians records the second letter that Paul writes to the church at Corinth. This devotional focuses on his words from the first chapter in verses three and four:

> *Praise be to the God and Father of our Lord Jesus Christ, the Father of compassion and the God of all comfort, who comforts us in all our troubles, so that we can comfort those in any trouble with the comfort we ourselves receive from God.*

Devotional thought: To experience the comfort of the Heavenly Father is indescribable. One night, in my darkest moment, when I believed all was lost, the Father gave me comfort; peace came upon me. What do I do with such an experience? Paul says to pass it on. Do you know someone in their darkest moment? Call them, visit them, invite them for lunch, or comfort them as you were comforted by the God of compassion. Today may be their darkest day, and you may be God's instrument of compassion and comfort in their life.

Prayer starter: Father, I know without a doubt that You give comfort when all seems lost, and I know others need You. Give me the heart to comfort the anxious, the hopeless, and those in need of peace.

2 Peter 1:16-18

Second Peter records the words of the apostle Peter written after Jesus' ascension into Heaven. It is written to the believers Peter had written to previously, confirming what they had been taught about Jesus. An excerpt from the first chapter in verses 16-18 reads as follows:

> *For we did not follow cleverly devised stories when we told you about the coming of our Lord Jesus Christ in power, but we were eyewitnesses of his majesty. He received honor and glory from God the Father when the voice came to him from the Majestic Glory saying, "This is my Son, whom I love; with him I am well pleased." We ourselves heard this voice that came from heaven when we were with him on the sacred mountain* (2 Peter 1:16-18).

Devotional thought: Peter, knowing his earthly life would soon be over, writes to the Christians about what he saw and heard—the transfiguration of Jesus on the mountain. Jesus' face shone like the sun, and his clothes were as white as the light. Also, there before Jesus were Moses and Elijah. They were talking with Jesus. Peter, James, and John were terrified. Jesus told them not to tell anyone of what they witnessed until His resurrection.

Have you ever had an experience like Peter, the kind where Jesus leads you up a high mountain, one that is difficult to climb? As you climb, do you wonder what Jesus is up to? But then, at the top of that mountain, Jesus reveals His greatness to you. You witness a moment of awe, wonder, and amazement. You finally understand what Jesus wanted you to learn and experience; you witnessed a moment like Peter did. But you don't need to keep this moment a secret. This time, Jesus is okay with you shouting the good news from the mountain top.

Prayer starter: Father, sometimes we wonder where we are being led, only to be amazed at what You wanted us to learn or experience. Let us share these moments with others so they will also be encouraged to continue their walk with You.

2 Peter 3:10-14

Part I

In Peter's second letter to the believers, he writes:

> *But the day of the Lord will come like a thief. The heavens will disappear with a roar; the elements will be destroyed by fire, and the earth and everything done in it will be laid bare. Since everything will be destroyed in this way, what kind of people ought you to be? You ought to live holy and godly lives as you look forward to the day of God and speed its coming. That day will bring about the destruction of the heavens by fire, and the elements will melt in the heat. But in keeping with his promise we are looking forward to a new heaven and a new earth, where righteousness dwells. So then, dear friends, since you are looking forward to this, make every effort to be found spotless, blameless and at peace with him* (2 Peter 3:10-14).

Devotional thought: How are we to be found spotless, blameless, and at peace with God? As most Christians know, it has nothing to do with human effort, for if we could be good enough to save ourselves with human effort, then Jesus died in vain. We know what the Bible says about humans: "All have sinned and have fallen short of the glory of God" (Romans 3:23). Without the blood of Jesus, all is lost. Man can try to be spotless, but only Jesus' sacrifice makes us that way.

Prayer starter: Dear Father, please help us to understand that we cannot be saved by our efforts. We are stained in sin without Jesus' sacrifice. Help us, Father, to understand what only You could do for us.

2 Peter 3: 10-14

Part II

In part one of this devotional thought, we read Peter's urging to the Christians to be spotless, blameless, and at peace with Him (God). Peter meant for those who are Christians to live a life in full obedience to God, being godly and holy. So, how are we to be found spotless and blameless? How can I be at peace with God?

Devotional thought: Let me make this suggestion: Peace with God starts with repenting. Peter says that God has not ended this Earth's existence because He is patient and wants everyone to repent (3:9). Isn't that an awesome thought, that the Creator may be forestalling His entire second coming for you or a loved one to come to repentance?

But what does repent really mean? Simply this: Cast off your old ways of living and give up the kingdom of self for the Kingdom of God. Instead of living in obedience to the world, begin living in obedience to the Creator—a complete 180-degree turn. Why is this important? Because you can't serve God and the world. You can't have two masters. So, repent! It's your choice. Who will you live for?

Prayer starter: Father, I want to quit living for the world and live for You. This world has gotten me nowhere. Life is a dead-end without You. I need more than this world has to offer. I need purpose. I need You. Help me live only for You.

2 Samuel 7

In 2 Samuel chapter 7, God made a promise to David that would last forever. David, King of the Israelites (God's chosen people), was living in a house of cedar while the Ark of God (God's dwelling place on Earth) was sheltered in a tent. David was determined to build God a temple to live in, but God told David through Nathan the prophet that he was not the one to build a temple for Him. David's son would be chosen for that task. Instead, God promised that David's house and kingdom would endure forever before Him.

Devotional thought: I love David's reply to God in verses 18-19:

> *Who am I Sovereign Lord, and what is my family, that you have brought me this far? And as if this were not enough in your sight, Sovereign Lord, you have also spoken about the future of the house of your servant – and this decree, Sovereign Lord, is for a mere human!*

David was in awe.

God's promise to us is this: *"For God so loved the world that he gave his one and only Son, that whoever believes in him shall not perish but have eternal life"* (John 3:16). The God and Creator of all sacrificed His only Son for mere humans that are full of selfishness, greed, jealousy, hate, lies, and the like. We should all fall to our knees in awe.

Prayer starter: Father, I am speechless! How can I, a mere human, express my gratitude for Jesus?

2 Timothy 2

2 Timothy is a letter from the apostle Paul to his co-worker, Timothy, written from a Roman prison. The letter was written to encourage Timothy when he was discouraged and intimidated. An excerpt from the second chapter in verse four reads: *"No one serving as a soldier gets entangled in civilian affairs, but rather tries to please his commanding officer."*

Devotional thought: The apostle Paul is writing to Timothy. In this verse, Paul tells Timothy to join him in suffering like a good soldier and not become so involved in worldly affairs. As I reflect on this, I think of how easy it is to get pushed off course. Worldly and local news tend to distract. Most things we cannot control, so efforts to do so usually fail. Frustration and anger set in, and we continue to stray off the path of eternal hope that is just around the corner. God knows the challenges of living on Earth. He lived among us and knows how easy it is to get distracted and veer off course, but His focus never wavered from God's eternal plan. If we get so involved with all that is happening around us, we will lose focus on the eternal. We will stray from God's plan for us. Stay the course. Focus on God.

Prayer starter: Dear Father, I am Your child, and I am here to serve You. I cannot serve the world and remain focused on the eternal. Help me to see the futility in trying.

2 Timothy 4

Later in his second letter to Timothy, Paul tells him, "…I give you this charge: Preach the word; be prepared in season and out of season; correct, rebuke and encourage – with great patience and careful instruction" (2 Timothy 4:1-2).

Devotional thought: Paul is directing Timothy on how to be effective to those in which he ministers. Timothy wasn't preaching and teaching to a flawless audience. They had their problems. Imposters, false teachers, and the like were trying to infiltrate the church, not to mention the everyday issues that occur in the church. Without a doubt, Timothy had his hands full. Each day presented new challenges. Paul tells Timothy to have great patience and give careful instruction. This advice is beneficial to all who teach, correct, and encourage. Great patience and careful instruction must be priorities for all who raise children, not to mention the patience God exhibits toward each of us. So, as you work with friends or family, rebuke, correct, and encourage with great patience and careful instruction. If you work with them the same way Paul instructs Timothy to work, then those needing such help will see the beauty of your Christian life, and you will be seen as caring and loving. Trust will grow, and progress will come.

Prayer starter: Dear Father, people can sense our anger or our love as we assist them in their walk. Let us display great patience with careful instruction as we minister to others.

A Believing Child

The first three books in the New Testament of the Bible mention a story about a millstone. A millstone was a cylinder-shaped heavy stone used in a mill for grinding grain. The story concerning the millstone tells about punishment for those who cause a believing child to sin. Here is what Jesus says about this:

> *...but whoever causes one of these little ones who believe in me to sin, it would be better for him to have a great millstone fastened around his neck and be drowned in the depth of the sea* (Matthew 18:6).

Devotional thought: How would one cause a believing child to sin? There are many ways—some in secret, which God will deal with severely, and others in plain sight such as to hinder or deny a child the spiritual food they need for their faith to grow. Oh, how terrible for one to cause a child to stumble! *"It would be better for them to have a great millstone fastened around their neck and be drowned in the depths of the sea."*

Parents, grandparents, teachers, elders, and guardians, give children the spiritual food they need regularly and take them to worship where believers can encourage them. Show them and tell them of our great God and what He did for us through Jesus' sacrifice on the cross. Study Deuteronomy 6:4-9, and let us live it.

Prayer starter: Father, as a parent, open my eyes to my responsibilities. Give me wisdom in supporting my child's precious faith.

A Reminder About Forgiving

Luke tells us in his gospel of a time that Jesus was eating dinner with a Pharisee, an expert in the law. As they were reclining at the table, a sinful woman came into the Pharisee's house and knelt behind Jesus. She began to weep bitterly, and her tears fell upon the feet of Jesus. With the tears that fell from her eyes, she washed Jesus' feet, a custom of the time that the host would normally provide for travelers, and she wipes them with her hair. She then poured expensive perfume on the master's feet. The Pharisee was appalled. Then, Jesus tells the Pharisee a story: A man loaned money to two people. One loan was 500 pieces of silver, and the other loan was 50 pieces of silver. Neither man could repay their loan, but the lender forgave both debtors. Then, Jesus posed this question to the Pharisee: "Which debtor will love the lender more?"

The Pharisee replied, "I suppose the one who had the bigger debt forgiven."

Jesus replied, "You have judged correctly."

Devotional thought: Our many sins have been freely forgiven. In turn, our love for Jesus should be beyond measure. Jesus took our place of punishment on the cross. He suffered the wrath of God for mankind's sins. Ours is the biggest debt of all – the wage of sin is death *forever.* Yet God forgave us! Therefore, our love for the Lender should be vast, and we should extend that to others.

Prayer starter: Father, when I fall into sin, You always forgive me. Give me the heart to always forgive others just as You do.

Acts 4

The book of Acts is the second book that Luke wrote after his gospel. It records the deeds of the first-century church. Chapter 4 in verse 12 reads, *"Salvation is found in no one else, for there is no other name under heaven given to mankind by which we must be saved."*

Devotional thought: During a discussion with the teachers of the law and elders about a lame man who was healed, Peter (an apostle of Jesus) takes the opportunity to tell this important fact to these rulers of the Israelites in Jerusalem: *"Salvation is found in no one else, for there is no other name under heaven given to mankind by which we must be saved."* The bottom line is this: Jesus of Nazareth died for your sins and was buried, and then God raised Him to sit at His right hand.

There is no need to pray to anyone else or argue with anyone about where your allegiance belongs. If you are Christian, your allegiance is to Christ. Pray to the Father through Jesus Christ our mediator.

Anyone besides Jesus is only a human. Your very salvation, your only hope, is in Christ.

Prayer starter: Heavenly Father, I am so thankful You have revealed that only in Jesus do we have any hope of salvation. Let my mission be to tell the lost that only in Christ we are saved.

Afflicted

The writer of the book of Hebrews states the following:

> *God disciplines us for our good, in order that we may share in his holiness. No discipline seems pleasant at the time, but painful. Later on, however, it produces a harvest of righteousness and peace for those who have been trained by it* (Hebrews 12:10-11).

Devotional thought: This verse paints a picture in my mind of God and Jesus looking down on me in my younger days. The Father then says to Jesus, "I've had about enough of him. Things are fixing to change." Woe to us that fully know God's ways yet ignore them. I promise one thing: Our Heavenly Father can get our attention quickly and will afflict us in ways that are unimaginable if that's what it takes to get our attention. The writer of Psalm chapter 119 must have experienced the discipline of God as well. Verse 67 states, *"Before I was afflicted I went astray, but now I obey your word."* Verse 71 states, *"It was good for me to be afflicted so that I might learn your decrees."* Verse 75 states, *"I know, Lord, that your laws are righteous, and that in faithfulness you have afflicted me."*

Sometimes it takes affliction, discipline, and punishment to wake us up and pay attention to the direction of our lives. As the Hebrew writer says, it is never "pleasant at the time," but those lessons can stick with us and guide our lives toward the path of righteousness, the path that leads us back to God.

Prayer starter: Father, thank You for Your discipline. Thank You for not giving up on us until You have it Your way. The affliction brought upon us now is our blessing later.

Aroma

One weekend, several members from my church and I went on a fishing trip to the Guadalupe River. We had good fortune and caught some whoppers. After the catch, it was time for the work to begin, and these exhausted yet determined and faithful fishermen found themselves cleaning fish for over three hours that night. With this accomplished, one question remained: What do we do with the intestines and all the other "gooey" stuff?

I pondered the thought of "donating" these contents to a local dumpster or my neighbor's trash can, but my conscience got the better of me. So, I "manned up" and placed my trash in my *own* trash can (which I keep by the street) until the following Thursday when our sanitation workers came.

Oh, my! Every hour of every day, the stench became worse. I found myself gagging when I went to retrieve the day's mail and when backing out of the driveway.

Devotional thought: This situation reminds me of politics; with disgusting politics comes a disgusting odor. You know the kind, right, the kind that makes you want to vomit? Most politicians have lost touch with the people. They haven't a clue what they represent or who they represent. They have forgotten their purpose. I have judged politicians harshly by their contrasting words and deeds, but how would God view my life in comparison? Have I become so self-centered and preoccupied with worldly events and cares that my spirituality and faithfulness have rotted? Have I forgotten who I vowed to represent, the Lord God Almighty? Could it be that when God walks by and searches me, He has this irresistible urge to vomit because of the contents of my heart? I am serious.

Prayer starter: Almighty, help me to get real. Revive me! Change me! My desire is to reflect You each day, that I may be a pleasing aroma in Your presence.

Ask, Seek, and Knock

Devotional thought: I am convinced that everyone who says, "There is no God" has not taken the time to honestly "Ask, Seek, and Knock" for the truth. God gives good gifts. His Spirit uncovers hidden mysteries and obscured certainties concerning Him. The Lord himself says:

> *Ask and it will be given to you; seek and you will find; knock and the door will be opened to you. For everyone who asks receives; the one who seeks finds; and to the one who knocks, the door will be opened* (Luke 7:9).

Since God does not lie, I guarantee that any unbeliever will find God when they honestly search. Their life will be changed forever. God makes this promise.

Prayer starter: Father, open our hearts and minds that we may hear You when we truly seek You.

Baptism

Baptism is a controversial subject among many; however, the first Christians understood the message clearly.

Devotional thought: The New Testament book of Acts is most enlightening when it comes to the subject of baptism. The writer of this book, Luke, records the beginning of the early church. Jews and non-Jews had come to believe in Jesus as the Son of God, the Christ, and the Savior of the world. Throughout this book, there is one thing in common with those who came to believe – they were baptized. The following are two of the many examples recorded in the book of Acts concerning the belief in Jesus as God's son and being baptized: Peter, in Acts chapter 2, tells the people of Israel all about the prophecies concerning Jesus and that they had crucified the Son of God. Luke says they were "cut to the heart" and asked what they should do? Peter replied, *"Repent and be baptized every one of you in the name of Jesus Christ for the forgiveness of your sins and you will receive the gift of the Holy Spirit"* (Acts 2:38).

Later in this book of Acts in chapters 21 and 22, Paul tells the story of his conversion to the courts while he was under arrest in Jerusalem. Paul did not believe that Jesus was the Son of God and severely fought against the early church. This wonderful story tells of how this unbeliever came to believe and was baptized.

See, it's simple. Don't get caught up in human traditions and arguments concerning baptism. They are never-ending. Just follow the first examples of those who came to believe in Jesus; they believed, then they were baptized.

Prayer starter: Dear Father, help us to see Your instructions. They are not difficult or confusing. Give us the wisdom to follow our brothers and sisters of the first church. The message was clear to them. Let it be clear to us.

Calloused Hearts

You will ever be hearing but never understanding; you will ever be seeing but never perceiving. For this people's heart has become calloused; they hardly hear with their ears, and they have closed their eyes. Otherwise they might see with their eyes, hear with their ears, understand with their hearts and turn, and I would heal them (Matthew 13:14-15).

Devotional thought: Approximately 700 years before the birth of Christ, Isaiah prophesied about the people of Israel in Jesus' time. Jesus quoted the prophet's words as recorded by Matthew, the apostle, in response to his disciples' question, *"Why do you speak to the people in parables?"* (Matthew 13:10).

They hear and see, but most do not understand and perceive. The path from the ears and eyes does not connect to the heart. The hearts of the Israelites were so calloused, they could not recognize the obvious: The long-awaited Messiah who came to heal them.

Could this prophesy say the same for us today? If we turn and repent, God will heal. I want you to examine your heart. Is it connected to God? Do you hear and see only what you want, or do you perceive and understand what God wants? God is ready to heal you. Turn to Him wholeheartedly. You will not be disappointed, I promise!

Prayer starter: Father, give us Your wisdom. Open our eyes and ears so that our hearts may truly perceive and understand who You are.

Caring

In the New Testament book of Mark chapter 2, there is a story about a paralyzed man at Capernaum. Jesus was teaching in someone's home, and people were pressing in close to get within seeing distance of Him. After all, news about Jesus had spread all over Galilee and beyond.

Four men were carrying one of their numbers, a paralyzed man, on a mat between them. They were trying to get him into the presence of Jesus, the Healer. The house was full to the point where people were spilling out, and people were standing in the doorway. Four men carrying someone on a mat requires a lot of room. The crowd wasn't budging. With no way to get the paralyzed man through the door, they devised another plan. But they needed to act quickly because Jesus could have left at any time. Those four men carried the paralyzed man onto the roof of the home in which Jesus was teaching. Then, making an opening in the roof by digging through it, they lowered this man in front of Jesus. Seeing their faith, Jesus said to the paralyzed man, *"Son, your sins are forgiven"* (Mark 2:5).

Devotional thought: This story is about Jesus and how He emphasizes to the crowd that He has the authority to forgive sins, but I also want to comment on those who carried the paralyzed man. The Bible does not identify those four men as his friends, but I don't think it would be a stretch to say they were associates. With all my heart, I hope you have friends like the paralyzed man. If so, treasure them. Those friends demonstrate love. Such friends are patient with you. They will pray with you, cry with you, and laugh with you. Yes, they would even carry you onto a roof if necessary. Your friends are living out what Jesus commands: "Love one another."

Prayer starter: Heavenly Father, thank You for my friends. In them I see Jesus.

Live a Life Worthy

"For Christ suffered once for sin, the righteous for the unrighteous, to bring you to God" (1 Peter 3:18).

"In him we have redemption through his blood, the forgiveness of sins, in accordance with the riches of God's grace that he lavished on us" (Ephesians 1:5-8).

"I urge you then to live a life worthy of the calling you have received" (Ephesians 4:1).

Devotional thought: If someone died for you, would you not honor them? If someone gave their life to save yours, would you not live in such a way as to make their sacrifice mean something? If someone breathed their last breath with your name upon their lips, would you not think of them every second of every day? Then why aren't you doing this? For this is exactly what has already come to pass!

Jesus, the Son of God, gave up His lofty position in Heaven to descend to the Earth. He mingled with lowly humans in the dust and the dirt to teach us the holy ways of righteousness. Then, we rejected Him, and we crucified Him. But He loved us so much that He went through with His plan from before the beginning of time and suffered and died on a cruel cross for all the world's sinners—all the world's sinners and me, me personally. God loves me. Jesus loves me. And the Holy Spirit is granted to me and lives in me when I accept this sacrifice and turn my life completely over to the one who died for me and you.

Jesus died for you not so that you could continue to fret over the worries of this life, but so that you can begin your life anew with Him, right now. Do not allow yourself to be weighed down by trials and suffering or your heart to be infiltrated by sin. Through Jesus' sacrifice, you have been set free of the burdens of this life and have been blessed with the joy that comes from being a child of God. I urge you, then, to take the words of Ephesians 4:1 to heart and live your life in a way that honors Jesus' sacrifice.

Jesus died so that you might live with His peace as your companion. Go, therefore, unburdened by the struggles of this world to "live a life worthy" of the sacrifice he made for you.

Jesus died for you. Live like it.

Jesus rose for you. God is not dead.

Prayer starter: Lord, help me honor Jesus' sacrifice on the cross with every breath and act of my life. Help me lead by example and give others a reason to ask why my actions are far removed from the habits of the world. Let me live like You died for me.

Colossians 1:21-23

Part I of III

Emphasis on Verse 21

While Paul was a prisoner in Rome, he wrote to the believers in the city of Colossae. Colossae is located in modern-day Turkey. Paul had never met them but had heard from one of his workers that they had started being pressured into following Jewish law and were adding extra rules. Paul wrote to them to say, "When you've got Jesus, you've got it all!" Paul emphasized that all things are reconciled or reunited with God through the Son's death on the cross. This devotional and the two subsequent devotionals focus on Colossians chapter 1, verses 21-23:

> *Once you were alienated from God and were enemies in your minds because of your evil behavior.* But now he has reconciled you by Christ's physical body through death to present you holy in his sight, without blemish and free from accusation – if you continue in your faith, established and firm, and do not move from the hope held out in the gospel. This is the gospel you have heard and that has been proclaimed to every creature under heaven, and of which I, Paul, have become a servant.*

Devotional thought: To be alienated from God is a dreadful thing. Before the crucifixion of Christ, there was no way to be reconciled with or be made right with God. The Law of Moses (the Ten Commandments and the like) made us aware of sin, but no one could keep the law perfectly, therefore making us all lawbreakers. You see, lawbreakers (sinners) and God could not come together without the perfect redeemer, Jesus, who was on the horizon, yet to be born under the Star of David in Bethlehem.

Prayer starter: Our Father in Heaven, how great You are. We were once lost, like sheep without a shepherd. We were guilty, but You provided cleansing through Jesus. Thank You.

Colossians 1:21-23

Part II of III

Emphasis on Verse 22

Continuing the devotionals concerning Paul's letter to the Colossians with chapter 1 verse 22:

> *Once you were alienated from God and were enemies in your minds because of your evil behavior. But now he has reconciled you by Christ's physical body through death to present you holy in his sight, without blemish and free from accusation – if you continue in your faith, established and firm, and do not move from the hope held out in the gospel. This is the gospel you have heard and that has been proclaimed to every creature under heaven, and of which I, Paul, have become a servant.*

Devotional thought: Paul writes this to the Christian church in Colossae. I've thought about this verse a lot. My understanding of this verse is most important to my faith. It defines the whole purpose of God's action in Jesus: To save the lost. First of all, it's very important to understand that Paul is writing to Christians—those who have given their lives to God, those who have repented of their sins and been baptized into Christ for the forgiveness of their sins, and those who struggle with the flesh but rely on the blood of Jesus for cleansing. Being cleansed by the precious blood of Jesus means just that – I am clean. It does not mean that at one moment I'm blemish-free then five minutes later I am not. It does not mean that if I sin, I am "unreconciled" with God. That kind of thinking reflects the way of the Old Covenant. Consider the words of the writer of the book of Hebrews from chapter 10 verse 14, *"For by one sacrifice he has made perfect forever those who are being made holy."* I am cleansed forever before God. That is the grace of God.

Prayer starter: My Heavenly Father, I am beginning to understand the meaning of grace – once being soaked in sin, but now being made holy, without blemish, and free from accusation through the final sacrifice. Praise You, Father!

Colossians 1:21-23

Part III of III

Emphasis on Verse 23

Finishing the devotionals concerning Paul's letter to the Colossians with chapter 1 verse 23, this is the final installment in that section of devotional thoughts:

> *Once you were alienated from God and were enemies in your minds because of your evil behavior. But now he has reconciled you by Christ's physical body through death to present you holy in his sight, without blemish and free from accusation – <u>if you continue in your faith, established and firm, and do not move from the hope held out in the gospel. This is the gospel you have heard and that has been proclaimed to every creature under heaven, and of which I, Paul, have become a servant.</u>*

Devotional thought: In verse 23, the word "if" has enormous implications. What does "if you continue in your faith" mean? In the parable of the Prodigal Son in Luke 15:11-32, the two sons were "with" the Father. Later, the younger son walked away from his relationship with the Father. Jesus described the younger son as "lost" and even called him "dead." The younger son did not continue his walk with the Father. He took the way of the world.

"If" the younger son had not walked away from the Father, he would have continued in this Father-son relationship. We know the rest of this story. The younger son later comes to his senses and returns to the Father. Jesus then describes the younger son as "found" and "alive." Unfortunately, many don't return; they leave fellowship with the Father, never to return again. They have fallen into the ways of the world, the kingdom of "self," and they are not aware of its consequences. They are lost. They are without the Father.

When Paul says, "If you continue in your faith," he means for you to do your utmost to make every effort to remain in the Father. Cast off anything that hinders you from coming to Christ or remaining in Christ. Jesus says, *"If your right eye causes you to stumble, gouge it out and throw it away. It is better to lose one part of your body than for your whole body to be thrown into hell"* (Matthew 5:29). That's how serious falling away from the Father is to be taken.

Prayer starter: O, my God, give me Your wisdom so that I can make good decisions. When relying on self, I will fail. I need You, Father. I must confess that without You, my life is in disorder. Save me, O God!

Colossians 2

While Paul was a prisoner in Rome, he wrote to the believers in the city of Colossae. Colossae is located in modern-day Turkey. Paul had never met them but had heard from one of his workers that they had started being pressured into following Jewish law and were adding extra rules. Paul wrote to them to say, "When you've got Jesus, you've got it all!" Colossians 2:8 says: *"See to it that no one takes you captive through hollow and deceptive philosophy, which depends on human tradition and the basic principles of this world rather than on Christ."*

Devotional thought: From the beginning of Jesus' ministry to the present day, false teachers have proclaimed flawed philosophies concerning Jesus. This is what the apostle Paul says: he is the *"image of the invisible God"* (Colossians 1:15), and *"in Christ all the fullness of the Deity lives in bodily form,"* (Colossians 2:9). Jesus repeatedly says throughout Scripture that the Father (God) and he are one.

We have no foundation to stand on if we say God is too big to understand or this "God thing" is too difficult for any human to comprehend. In Jesus, we understand exactly what God wanted to disclose to us because all the fullness of God came to His people in Jesus. Jesus is God-made flesh. If we want to understand the

Father and His teachings, we need to look to the son, Jesus. Only in Jesus can we truly know God.

Prayer starter: Great Father, give us wisdom that comes only from You. Help us recognize the deception of those who wish to spoil our hope in You. Open our eyes to see who You truly are through Your son, Jesus Christ.

Commander

The Scripture that inspired this devotional thought comes from Job 38:11: "This far you may come and no farther; here is where your proud waves halt."

Devotional thought: As my wife, Nancy, and I visit the Texas coast, we are fortunate to sit on the beach and watch the waves roll in. I am reminded of God speaking to Job regarding creation. Concerning the sea in Job chapter 38 verse 11, God is asking Job where he was when God set limits on the waves, for God said to the waves, "This far you may come and no farther; here is where your proud waves halt."

Amazing!

The Creator and Commander of all things creates and gives limits to these vast ocean waves, commanding them to obey. This Creator is our Creator, too. He is at the beginning and the end of all things. He knows my every thought. Just as He created the waves, He also created us and will save us if only we accept Him and obey His commands.

Prayer starter: Maker of all, command my life as You commanded the waves during the creation. Be in control of my every thought and motive.

Comparison

In the Old Testament book of Exodus in chapters 19 and 20, the Lord descends upon Mount Sinai. It is there, upon the mountain summit, that the Ten Commandments were given to Moses. As the Lord descended upon the mountain, Moses put limits around the perimeter so that no person nor animal may get near Sinai. To do so meant death. This scene is majestic: The Lord descends, smoke billows, thunder and lightning erupt, a trumpet blasts, and the whole mountain shakes violently. The trumpet sound grows louder and louder. Moses speaks, and the voice of God answers him; the people tremble with fear!

In the New Testament book of Revelation, chapter 5, John describes this splendid scene: In the presence of God and Christ, angels numbering thousands upon thousands, and ten thousand upon ten thousand, as well as every creature on the Earth and under the earth and every creature in Heaven proclaim, *"To him who sits on the throne and to the Lamb be praise and honor and glory and power for ever and ever"* (Revelations 5:13).

Devotional thought: Today, as I meander into the church each Sunday morning, I sit in my seat and settle in. As I observe the people in this place of worship, one is constantly yawning, some are playing on their phones, others are eating their donuts and coffee, and I complain to myself that the temperature is not to my liking.

The thought of the Lord Himself in my presence never crosses my preoccupied mind. In my mind, I compare those three worship scenes, and I wonder what God would think. Would He accept our current level of distraction and routine approach to worship when He knows what it is to be truly praised? I think we already know the answer to this question if we look into our hearts.

Prayer starter: Forgive me, Father, for not preparing to be in Your presence. Move me to be in awe of Your greatness.

David Defeats the Giant

In the time of King Saul, long ago in the time before Christ, the Israelites (God's chosen people) faced off in battle against a people called the Philistines in the Valley of Elah. Even though they had God on their side, the Israelites were scared to go up against the Philistine champion, a giant of a man called Goliath—that is until a boy decided to have faith in God to protect him. When he challenged Goliath, David exclaimed, *"All those gathered here will know that it is not by sword or spear that the Lord saves; for the battle is the Lord's, and he will give all of you into our hands"* (1 Samuel 17:47).

Devotional thought: David, just older than a boy, tells Goliath that he will not die by the power of man's might, but by the power of the living God. Scripture says Goliath had come out against the army of Israel every day for a month. David's older brothers and the rest of the Israelite army saw Goliath as a problem that they had no answer for. But Israel had the problem: They were relying on their own strength and looking for something physical to defeat this giant. Odds are, no one from the Israelite army could have defeated such a battle-worthy opponent on their own.

What do you see when problems come upon you face to face? Do you see an impossible, unmanageable task? Do you bow your head in despair and say, "Oh, not again"? Do you want to get in bed, cover up, and wish it would go away? Perhaps your problems seem to never go away because, as the army of Israel, you only look to yourself and depend upon your own strength and process to defeat the "giant."

God did not want a mighty warrior from the army to defeat this fierce enemy. If that had happened, Israel would get to say, "Look what I did!" Instead, God chose the most unlikely person to defeat the most formidable. In other words, it was God who came to the rescue and is always victorious. God wants you to see that all things are only possible through Him.

Prayer starter: Father, we often ask for wisdom because, as humans, we believe we can defeat the undefeatable by ourselves. How foolish of us. May Your power prevail, and let us only give You the glory.

Debt

Devotional thought: When I think about the word "debt," it is a word that everyone is very familiar with on Earth. Debt follows us most of our adult life. Debt always finds us. It reaches us by mail, phone, and the occasional knock on the front door. It's probably a major reason most married couples argue and some divorce. Being submerged in debt means someone has a hold of your very way of life. It dictates when and where you go. It has a say in everything from what is in your freezer to what college your children may attend if any.

For most, debt is an unavoidable circumstance that is self-inflicted. Sadly, many will die still owing a debt to someone. This kind of debt will cease when death occurs.

Spiritually, we find ourselves in a similar circumstance. This kind of debt, though, is spiritual debt, and it is unavoidable. It touches all who have ever lived. For the majority, it is self-inflicted. It is unpayable by human effort and has an eternal consequence. This time, our debt does not cease when death occurs.

The only means to release us from this spiritual debt is by way of the Savior, Jesus. God saw, considered our pitiful condition, and paid the price by giving us the purest of sacrifices, Jesus Christ, the Son of God. With this sacrifice, we are cleansed and relieved of all debt; we are debt-free for life.

All mankind is stained with this debt called sin, but it has been paid for those who are His. Tragically, most will reject the Father's gift and will repay their debt by the punishment of eternal separation from God. Don't let this happen to you. Accept the Father's gift of a pure and blameless sacrifice that frees us from our debt of sin and live with Him in Heaven forever.

Prayer starter: Heavenly Father, I believe my debts have been paid through the blood of Jesus. Help me in rescuing those who are not yet aware of Jesus' sacrifice.

Deep and Wide

"And I pray that you being rooted and established in love, may have power, together with all the Lord's holy people, to grasp how wide and long and high and deep is the love of Christ, and to know this love that surpasses all knowledge – that you may be filled to the measure of all the fullness of God" (Ephesians 3:17-19).

When I was a child, I used to look forward to an event at my church every summer called Vacation Bible School, or VBS as we used to call it. Not a very enticing name for a kid, I'll admit, but once you went, you were hooked, or at least I was hooked. It was a few days, maybe even a week, where the church was covered in paper mâché, backdrops of ancient Hebrew cities, and mock-ups of Noah's ark. Church volunteers were decked out in their best approximations of "Bible-time" clothes, though wearing sandals with Velcro. My favorite parts were the songs, all the children's praise songs that we didn't sing in "regular" church service, those that had all the cool hand motions.

One song comes to mind called "Deep and Wide."

"Deep and wide, there's a fountain flowing deep and wide."

You would hold your hands about a foot apart vertically then horizontally to indicate deep then wide. The best part of the song, though some would say the worst, is that each successive verse would drop a word until you ended up humming the whole song. The verses from Ephesians 3:17-19 remind me of that song, though in a more meaningful way.

Devotional thought: In those verses, Paul prays with everything he has that Christ may dwell in our hearts and that we could somehow, someway come to understand just how much God loves us. What he is trying to get us to comprehend is that God's love is so big that it is beyond our capability to know. It is wide, long, high, and deep and like nothing we've ever known. That is how much God loves us. It is wider, longer, higher, and deeper than any love we've ever felt. In these verses, Paul is praying for the people, for us, to grasp the measure of God's love for us, as if that were possible for a human. To further define the undefinable, Paul goes on to wish that we "know this love that surpasses all knowledge." He specifically says that it "surpasses all knowledge." How can we know something that "surpasses all knowledge"? We can't! He wants us to get as close as humanly possible to knowing God's love, but it is so vast that we cannot wrap our heads around something so huge. *That* is how much God loves us, and it is amazing! It's like trying to count the stars. You can try to know how many there are, but at some point, you just have to say, "I'm never going to be able to count them all. There are a lot of them." It's the same with God's love. You can try to comprehend it, but at some point, you have to say, "God loves me more than I could ever fully understand. He loves me enough to die for me. He loves me wide, long, high, and deep."

Prayer starter: Lord, never allow me to give up trying to understand how much You love me. Help me to feel Your love with all my heart and to try to grasp just how wide and long and high and deep Your love is and to share that love with others.

Don't Panic

Devotional thought: The apostle Paul's ministry was fraught with hardship. As his days on Earth drew to a close, he wrote from prison to encourage Timothy, his co-worker, to stay faithful to the true message of God and not get discouraged or intimidated by those trying to undermine and oppose him. In the latter part of his letter, Paul said this to Timothy:

> *For the time will come when people will not put up with sound doctrine. Instead, to suit their own desires, they will gather around them a great number of teachers to say what their itching ears want to hear. They will turn their ears away from the truth and turn aside to myths. But you, keep your head in all situations, endure hardship, do the work of an evangelist, discharge all the duties of your ministry* (2 Timothy 4:3-5).

Amazing, isn't it?

I wonder how many times in history that Paul's words have been right on target. This century most certainly deserves consideration. Christians, keep your head in all situations. Don't let the events here, in our country or globally, overwhelm you. Paul and Jesus have forewarned us that things will get nasty. Trust in God. Let His peace be upon you. And let that peace allow you to continue in the good work of God—the duty of your ministry.

Prayer starter: Father, teach us to stay calm during this time of calamity. Help us to be examples of courage. When most are in fear or turning aside to false teachings, let us stand firm in You. God, You are awesome!

Eternal Fire

In the New Testament book of Matthew, Jesus describes the Kingdom of Heaven. He depicts it in many ways, but at the end of the chapter, Jesus reveals that all those who cared for the hungry, strangers, sick, and imprisoned will enter the Kingdom because whatever they did for the least of these, they did for Him. Yet, all those who ignore those outcasts received the opposite message in his next words, "*Then he will say to those on his left, 'Depart from me, you who are cursed, into the eternal fire prepared for the devil and his angels'*" (Matthew 25:41).

Devotional thought: Yes, there is a place of eternal fire just as there is a place of eternal life. Both have been prepared since the creation of the world. Yes, there is a judgment. It rapidly approaches. The sexually immoral, the greedy, the selfish, the God-haters, and the like will receive a judgment that is dreadful and infinite. Jesus tells the disciples early in his ministry: *"Many will say to me on that day, 'Lord, Lord, did we not prophesy in your name and in your name drive out demons and in your name perform many miracles?' Then the Lord tells them plainly, 'I never knew you'"* (Matthew 7:22-23).

My request to you: Please take a day to reflect on your devotion and your relationship with the Creator. If need be, do what you must to cast off acts of hate, greed, selfishness, and sexual immorality. Allow the Father to perform a complete overhaul upon you. Be honest with God. Be honest with yourself. Let Him change you. Let Him save you from the eternal fire. Peace be upon you.

Prayer starter: Father, we need Your wisdom. We have ears to hear, so please let us hear Your plea to turn our lives to You.

Faith and Deeds

James, one of the brothers of Jesus, became an influential leader in the Jerusalem church after Jesus' death and resurrection. His wisdom was respected and sought after to help make decisions among the people. Wanting to share his understanding of Jesus' teachings with his fellow believers, he wrote down some of his best advice and counsel sending it out to the Christians as a letter. Midway through his letter, James asks these bold questions, *"What good is it, my brothers and sisters, if someone claims to have faith but has no deeds? Can such faith save them?"* (James 2:14).

James continues his point in verses 15-16 by giving us this example:

> *Suppose a brother or sister is without clothes and daily food (a real possibility these days). If one of you says to them, 'Go in peace; keep warm and well fed,' but does nothing about their physical needs, what good is it?*

Devotional thought: What good is my faith in God if I *only* believe, if *all* I do is believe? What good is my belief if it consists only of "lip service"? James says it is dead and useless. In other words, it is of zero value. Sometimes, I think I pray in disrespect. As I awake each morning, I give God his "to-do list" while I go about my busy schedule that seems to always favor myself and my kingdom, not God's. I think about those in need and ask the Lord to bless them, but I do nothing about it. I am all faith and no deeds. I am all talk and no walk. What if God had said, "I'll send my son to save you," but never sent Him? What if I say to you, "I'll walk this mile with you," but I never take a step? James says that a person is justified by what they do, not by faith alone. He is saying to prove that you have faith by letting your life, your deeds, reflect it. *"Show me your faith without deeds, and I will show you my faith by my deeds"* (James 2:18).

Prayer starter: Father, please forgive me when I am lazy and expect You to do all my work. Revive my mind and heart and awaken my spirit that I may show my faith by the deeds I do in Your name.

Faith Part I

Devotional thought: If I rely on myself to generate my faith, then my faith can only be as strong as me. This type of behavior and thinking, relying only on myself, will perpetually keep my faith on a roller coaster causing unpredictable ups and downs. When I feel good about myself and life is on the level, my faith will follow, being strong and steadfast. The same goes for when I feel the opposite. When I am uneasy and vulnerable, my faith will follow as weak and wavering.

Do you see what is occurring? I'm using my human nature against me. When there is peace like a smooth river surface, I am all for God and never question Him, but when sorrows like sea billows roll (the great storms of life), I question God who I had praised. I may accuse God of not caring, or I may question His existence. I repeat, my faith is only as strong as me when I rely on myself for its origin. Unfortunately, many Christians never see this trap. They never recognize why their faith is tossed back and forth like waves in the wind. Maturing in faith eludes them because they rely on themselves instead of the Author and Perfecter of the faith. The writer of the Hebrew letter says, *"Fix your eyes on Jesus, the author and perfecter of faith"* (Hebrews 12:2).

Prayer starter: Father, give us Your wisdom that we may understand ourselves, for we are only flesh and blood.

Faith Part II

"Fix your eyes on Jesus, the author and perfecter of faith..." (Hebrew 12:2).

Devotional thought: Jesus knows my weaknesses. Therefore, He must do something to create in me a real faith so that I will be a true soldier, one that can withstand the battles of spiritual warfare. Jesus has to remove a lot of junk in us to replace it with real substance. He has to rid us of self-learned faith, what we thought faith really was, to replace it with real faith. Once Jesus sees that the timing is right, He will begin His work in us.

I lost my faith once, or so I thought. I could neither prove nor disprove the Creator's existence. I was ashamed, embarrassed, humiliated, and horrified at the same time. The more I tried to prove God's existence, the more Satan countered. The deceiver was winning. I thought, "My God, what is happening to me?" I turned to my best friend, Robert Barkley, for help. The following is an excerpt from his book, *Looking for God*:

Faith is not self-confidence or positive thinking. It begins as just the opposite. Real faith starts at the point where I say, God, I can't do it. I give up. I'm turning it all over to you and trusting you completely. Only faith that is complete surrender will allow God to transform your life. The harder a person tries to be a winner, the less sure he is that he has won. The person who surrenders can know for sure that he has surrendered. The first has a false confidence. The second knows he has surrendered and comes to have great confidence, not in himself, but in his new boss. Through surrender, he becomes a conqueror. The paradox of winning and losing is this: the one who tries to win ultimately loses; the one who surrenders ultimately wins (Barkley, 2013).

This I did, and God won.

Prayer starter: Dear God, thank You for trials that defeat me but that You conquer. Only through surrender to You can true faith and peace be obtained.

Falling Away

In the passage leading up to our devotional verses, the writer of Hebrews admonishes his audience because they should be farther along in their faith. Instead, he is having to reteach them the fundamentals of Christianity. He mockingly says in chapter 5 verse 12: *"You need milk, not solid food,"* equating them to babies in the faith. The Hebrew writer urges the people to move beyond elementary teachings, go deeper into their faith, and not fall away. He then goes on to define what falling away looks like and what it really means.

That's where we pick up with the key verses for our devotional, beginning in Hebrews 6: 4-6:

> *It is impossible for those who have once been enlightened, who have tasted the heavenly gift, who have shared in the Holy Spirit, who have tasted the goodness of the word of God and the powers of the coming age and who have fallen away, to be brought back to repentance. To their loss they are crucifying the Son of God all over again and subjecting him to public disgrace.*

Devotional thought: Many scholars believe the Hebrew writer meant that many early Christians considered abandoning the faith because of severe persecution. The early Christians could avoid this persecution if they reverted back to Judaism. Regardless of the exact reason for this warning, today's Christians must also be on guard of falling away and potentially suffering the same judgment.

To clarify: This is not a matter of everyday sin or occasional failings but a serious "fall," arrogantly rejecting the value of Christ's sacrifice. Two thousand and some years later, the devil is as alive today as he was in the church in its early years. Back then, persecution was a major contributor to people leaving the church. Our persecution is different, and our struggles are different, but their fate and our fate remain in God's hands.

What is the excuse of so many today for leaving the church and abandoning their faith? Here is what Jesus says: *"Because of the increase in wickedness, the love of most will grow cold, but the one who stands firm to the end will be saved"* (Matthew 24:12). As Peter says, *"Be alert and of sober mind. Your enemy the devil prowls around like a roaring lion looking for someone to devour"* (1 Peter 5:8). My plea to each of you is this: Stand firm to the end!

Prayer starter: Heavenly Father, give us Your wisdom. We ask You to help us stand firm until You return.

Forgiven Much

As discussed in an earlier devotional, Luke tells us in his gospel of a time that Jesus was eating dinner with a Pharisee, an expert in the law. As they were reclining at the table, a sinful woman came into the Pharisee's house and knelt behind Jesus. She began to weep bitterly, and her tears fell upon the feet of Jesus. With the tears that fell from her eyes, she washed Jesus' feet, a custom of the time that the host would provide for travelers, and wiped them with her hair. She then poured expensive perfume on the master's feet. The Pharisee was appalled. Then, Jesus told the Pharisee a story: A man loaned money to two people. One loan was 500 pieces of silver, and the other was 50 pieces of silver. Neither man could repay the loan, but the moneylender forgave both debtors. Then, Jesus posed this question to the Pharisee: *"Which debtor will love the lender more?" The Pharisee replied, "I suppose the one who had the bigger debt forgiven." Jesus replied, "You have judged correctly"* (Luke 7:41-43).

Devotional thought: This woman, who is thought to be a prostitute, is also at Simon's house, the Pharisee. She knows that the Pharisee looks at her way of life as despicable, wicked, and shameful. In front of Jesus is a man who belongs to a religious group called the Pharisees. Pharisees are known to keep the letter of the Jewish religious law to perfection, or so they think. They are often portrayed by Jesus as self-righteous, self-centered, and proud, clean on the outside, filthy on the inside, and showing no mercy to sinners. The Pharisees believe they are near to God because of their actions. The Pharisees claim that keeping the letter of the law brings perfection and justification. They believe they are in little need of forgiveness because their sins are of little significance. Behind Jesus kneels this sinful woman. She is ashamed of her way of living. She is well aware that the Pharisees look upon her like the scum of the Earth because of her outward sin. The woman believes she is far from the grace of God because of her actions. Her guilt weighs heavily upon her. Her heart is broken. Her emotions well up and she is speechless in the presence of the Master. She weeps bitterly. This sinful woman throws herself at the mercy of Jesus for she is ready for change. She knows she is in need of much forgiveness. Jesus is asking, "Who will love me more?" Will it be the one who looks at himself with pride and sees himself justified by his own actions or the one who says, 'Lord, have mercy on me, a sinner'? The latter loves Jesus more, for theirs is the greater debt, and they are the very ones that Jesus calls to Himself.

Note the words of Jesus recorded in the New Testament book of Matthew in chapter 11 verse 28: *"Come to me, all of you who are weary and burdened, and I will give you rest."*

Prayer starter: Heavenly Father, thank You for canceling my debt through the blood of Jesus. I love You much, for You have forgiven much. My love and gratitude are like the sinful woman's, more than I can express in words.

Forgiving

The apostle John, one of Jesus' chosen 12, shares God's viewpoint on forgiveness and love with his readers. It is recorded in one of John's letters in the New Testament. It reads as follows:

> *Whoever claims to love God yet hates a brother or sister is a liar. For whoever does not love their brother or sister, whom they have seen, cannot love God whom they have not seen. And he has given this command: Anyone who loves God must also love their brother and sister* (1 John 4:20-21).

Devotional thought: When we remember the sins we committed and realize how far we had fallen from God, it is terrifying. The repentant Christians can only bow their heads in awe of God's grace and forgiveness. Only after we grasp this full measure of forgiveness, which was so freely given to us, can we then stop our hating of others.

Prayer starter: My God, help me, a forgiven transgressor, to forgive others as You forgive me. I was lost and was found. I was dead and made alive.

Galatians 6:1

In his letter to the Galatians, Paul strives to emphasize that followers of Christ are no longer under the old law but under the New Covenant of grace and mercy. Still, he outlines in previous verses, *"the flesh desires what is contrary to the Spirit, and Spirit what is contrary to the flesh. They are in conflict with each other, so that you are not to do whatever you want"* (Galatians 5:17).

Therefore, even though we are not under the strict law of the Old Covenant, we are to walk by the Spirit and not act on the desires of the flesh—do not sin. In accordance with that, we are to help our fellow Christians in this endeavor. Paul says in Galatians 6:1, *"Brothers and sisters, if someone is caught in a sin, you who live by the Spirit should restore that person gently."*

Devotional thought: Just a few verses earlier, Paul defines what the Spirit produces in us. The fruit of the Spirit enables us to have *"love, joy, peace, patience, kindness, goodness, faithfulness, gentleness, and self-control"* (Galatians 5:22-23). These characteristics should be displayed by Christians every day for all to see. Such characteristics are to be used as a measuring stick to size up our spiritual growth.

When a brother or sister falls and crashes (caught in sin), how should they respond?

Repentantly.

How should we respond to that repentant brother or sister?

In gentleness.

If a brother or a sister is truly in Christ and stumbles because of sin, then it is the job of fellow Christians to show them the error of their ways and instruct them in the way they should go with love and gentleness.

Prayer starter: Dear Father, correcting others can be difficult. Strengthen my innermost being so I can forgive them as You forgave me. My scars are evidence that I, too, have fallen. Thank You for restoring me gently.

Hebrews 2

The writer of the Hebrew letter says in chapter 2 verse 1, *"We must pay the most careful attention, therefore, to what we have heard, so that we do not drift away."* The Hebrew writer is admonishing the Jewish converts to Christianity not to do as their ancestors often did and turn away from God's teachings. In Old Testament times, the consequences for this were that the earthly kingdom of Israel was overrun by a more powerful earthly enemy. In the New Covenant, the way of Jesus, the consequences are much more dire; your soul is at risk, not just your life.

Devotional thought: The Almighty has seen to it that we have heard the absolute truth concerning our Savior Jesus: God was before time; He created then came to the Earth He made in the Messiah Jesus who lived among mankind, offered Himself as the last sacrifice for sin, was crucified, and buried and then God raised Him from the dead on the third day; Jesus then ascended to Heaven and is now at the right hand of God. Those truths are absolute. Keep those truths at the forefront of your life and you will not drift. Drifting means giving up your soul. Jesus died for you. Live like it!

Prayer starter: Your Holy Spirit has revealed to us Your most important truths. Keep us close so that we never drift and exchange those truths for the world's temptations.

Hebrews 3

The writer of Hebrews, though not specifically named, speaks truth to the Jesus-believing Jews in danger of falling away from faith. The writer's goal is to show the superiority of the New Covenant in Jesus over the Old Covenant in Moses. In the third chapter, the Hebrew writer makes a point to name our God as the "living God." Hebrews 3:12-13 reads:

> *See to it, brothers and sisters, that none of you has a sinful, unbelieving heart that turns away from the living God. But encourage one another daily, as long as it is called "Today," so that none of you may be hardened by sin's deceitfulness.*

Devotional thought: The author of this letter warned the Jewish converts to Christianity not to revert back to Judaism. Turning away from Christianity means turning away from the living God. Even today, some trade the living God for a dead idol— self-love, money, power, and status. As the writer says, they are "hardened by sin's deceitfulness. "

What did "sin's deceitfulness" mean then? To the recipients of this letter, it meant that instead of enduring persecution and remaining in Christ, they listened to the false teachers trying to persuade them to return to the Law of Moses. It meant taking the easy road and falling back on tradition. Some would leave the mercy and grace that God had so graciously given them in Jesus to return to the Law through which reconciliation with God was impossible.

What does "sin's deceitfulness" mean today? To the Christian today, it means surrendering to anyone who would deceive you with empty words which would hinder your obedience to Christ, our Savior, and submitting to anything that would stand in the way of living for Christ who now saves you. Today, it means giving up the living God for our selfish desires—things that may look appealing but lead us far from salvation.

So, encourage one another daily, not only with words of truth but acts of compassion. In all we do, do it for the sake of Christ Jesus, who gave His life for our sins.

Prayer starter: Father, let us continually be on guard against the devil's schemes. May all they accomplish glorify You and not self.

Hebrews 4

Hebrews 4:13: *"Nothing in all creation is hidden from God's sight. Everything is uncovered and laid bare before the eyes of him to whom we must give account."*

Devotional thought: The Hebrew writer preludes this verse with one that describes the Word of God as being "sharper than any double-edged sword," able to divide thoughts and attitudes, judging the soul. The writer of Hebrews is talking to Jewish converts to Christianity. These people know the Scriptures of how God spoke the world into existence. The God that can do that is not ignorant of your sins just because you do them behind closed doors. The Hebrew writer gives us great insight into what we must answer to God for. He warns us that all things are laid bare before the Lord Almighty.

The deepest secrets from our innermost being, a place where no one is allowed to enter but you, are uncovered and laid completely bare before the eyes of our God. Not only is nothing hidden from the Creator, but we will also be required to give an account to Him for all things.

This opens our eyes to the reality that our secrets are no longer so secret. Honestly, they never were. I hope that motivates you. I hope that Hebrews 4:13 moves you to be honest with yourself and God.

When you truly confess to the Almighty all that is deep inside your soul, it will bring forth an indescribable feeling of true peace.

Prayer starter: Cleanse my heart, O God, and change my life. Please, forgive me in the name of Jesus.

Humanity

Devotional thought: Genesis 1:1 – In the beginning, God created…

Paul, while on a missionary journey through Rome, told those in Athens that God gives us *"life, breath and everything else,"* and that through God, *"we live and move and have our being"* (Acts 17:16-34).

Amazing, isn't it?

The all-knowing God who knew we would sin even before the creation of the world created us anyway and then rescues us from the dominion of darkness with the power of the Resurrected Christ.

Prayer starter: My Savior and my God; Father, thank You!

James 1

Temptation

James, the brother of Christ, became a leader of the church in Jerusalem. In his teaching ministry, he defined what it is to sin and the consequences of sin. James 1:14-15:

> *Each person is tempted when they are dragged away by their own evil desire and enticed. Then, after desire has conceived, it gives birth to sin; and sin, when it is full grown, gives birth to death.*

Devotional thought: Temptation should be avoided like a deadly virus. Temptation in conjunction with evil desires is a perfect recipe for sin to get a foothold. When my evil desires become enticed by coming in close proximity to things that I know will push me over the edge, it's like throwing gasoline on a flame, creating a blazing inferno. In this case, sin becomes full grown. Sin, like fire, must be quickly extinguished before death occurs. I recognize temptation on a daily basis. You know the type—sexual immorality, greed, hatred, gossip, jealousy, and the like. You may struggle with one type of temptation; I struggle with another. They all lead to sin if we let them go unchecked, and then sin leads to spiritual death, the separation from God. Flee from temptation as you would a virus. It's like a hidden bomb, ready to consume the unwise.

Prayer starter: Dear Heavenly Father, please help us in our weakness, as each one of us faces temptations daily. Give us swift feet to flee.

James 1

In the letter of James, the brother of Jesus, he opens with this familiar passage: *"Consider it pure joy my brothers and sisters whenever you face trials of many kinds..."* (James 1:2).

Devotional thought: James does not say *if* trouble comes your way but *when* it does. He assumes we will have troubles and it is possible to grow from them. We will face pain. Therefore, we must comprehend the realities of living in a dark and corrupted world. This pain will produce a perpetual whiner that remains perplexed at why life is always against them, or the pain will produce perseverance, character, and matureness as God desires. We must come to terms with living in a dark world. This is not our home. Our home is with the Lord in Heaven when our trials on Earth are through.

Prayer starter: Dear Father, give me Your wisdom. Help me to always see that Earth is not my final place.

Jehoshaphat

Part I

In 2 Chronicles chapter 20, there is a story of the King of Judah and how he overcame a great and overwhelming army. There are lessons we can learn from this awesome story to help us overcome trials in our earthly life.

Jehoshaphat, King of Judah, was a man of God. He tried to lead Judah away from worshipping idols and foreign gods and protect Judah from invading armies. Even though Jehoshaphat tried to please God, trials still came his way. 2 Chronicles 20:2-3 reads:

> *Some people came and told Jehoshaphat, "A vast army is coming against you from Edom, from the other side of the Dead Sea. It is already in Hazezon Tamar" (that is, En Gedi). Alarmed, Jehoshaphat resolved to inquire of the Lord, and he proclaimed a fast for all Judah.*

Devotional thought: Like Jehoshaphat, a vast army can quickly come against you without warning. This fast-approaching enemy can take any shape—loss of job, poor health, divorce, loss of a loved one, etc. When this fast-approaching army is made known to you, I hope your reaction is the same as Jehoshaphat's. He inquired of the Lord, the only One who could defeat such an enemy. Jehoshaphat's priority was to put all other issues of running a kingdom on hold and come to God immediately. Our priority should be the same.

Prayer starter: Father, we never know whether good or bad is around the corner. Whatever shows its face, let us inquire of You without delay, for You are the Almighty God.

Jehoshaphat

Part II

Continuing our focus on Jehoshaphat, we see that as the enemy army approaches, he stood up in the assembly of Judah and prayed. An excerpt of his prayer from 2 Chronicles 20:9 reads:

> *If calamity comes upon us, whether the sword of judgment, or plague or famine, we will stand in your presence before this temple that bears your Name and will cry out to you in our distress, and you will hear us and save us.*

Devotional thought: Verse 9 is only a small piece of Jehoshaphat's prayer. However, in this verse, Jehoshaphat is honest with himself and God as to what may be the outcome of facing such a vast army. Jehoshaphat is praying that no matter the outcome of this calamity if sword or plague comes upon him and Judah, they are determined to continue their appeal to God until He delivers them from this enemy that has come against them.

Never let what appears to be defeat stop you from praying to God for deliverance. God has the final say regarding all things. Jehoshaphat knew this, for he said he will continue to cry out, and God will hear and save. The Lord has power over sin and the grave.

Prayer starter: Father, Jehoshaphat knew that all things are in Your hands. Help us to be faithful as he, knowing that You can deliver even in the darkest moments of calamity.

Jehoshaphat

Part III

As Jehoshaphat completed his prayer to God concerning this large and fast-approaching army coming against him, notice Jehoshaphat's surrendering words. He says to God, *"For we have no power to face this vast army that is attacking us. We do not know what to do, but our eyes are on you"* (2 Chronicles 20:12).

Devotional thought: Before I was taught better, I spent many hours trying to solve problems I had no power over. After years of God teaching me, I can now say that I am more likely to be like Jehoshaphat. I simply admit I have no power to defeat or solve what has come against me. Instead, my eyes are upon God.

As mentioned before, genuine faith is not about being self-determined and trying to plow through the trials to solve your issues. Genuine faith is the opposite. It is depending on God to see you through what appears to be the impossible. In complete surrender to the Creator, we find our peace.

Prayer starter: Our Heavenly Father, give us Your wisdom. Help us to repent of trying to be self-reliant but, instead, take the road of Jehoshaphat when he said, "We don't know what to do, but our eyes are upon you."

Jehoshaphat

Part IV

During what appeared to be probable doom for Judah when the arrival of a hoard of enemy warriors was eminent, Jehoshaphat, along with all the men of Judah, with their wives and children and little ones, stood before the Lord. Then, the Spirit of the Lord came upon a man named Jahaziel, and he proclaimed this to the assembled people of God: *"Do not be afraid or discouraged because of this vast army. For the battle is not yours, but God's"* (2 Chronicles 20:15).

Earlier in Israel's history, God could have annihilated this assembled army from Amon, Moab, and Mount Seir. Instead, He allowed them to remain. Years later, this army was on the march, ready to destroy Jehoshaphat along with all of Judah. Jehoshaphat had nothing to do with the history of this event. Unfortunately for him, this vast destructive army became his problem. He needed direction. To whom shall he turn?

Devotional thought: Like Jehoshaphat, we may find ourselves in similar circumstances. Some event from the past that you are innocent of now comes to rest upon you. To whom shall you turn?

Jehoshaphat had a powerful army, but it was no match for what was coming against him. Similarly, we have the means to resolve some problems in our lives, but others are impossible to neutralize. God sees this. Maybe He's saying to you, "This fight is not yours. I'll take care of it."

Later in this story, God utterly destroys and annihilates this enemy to the very last man. God can do the same with "armies" that stand against you. God is mighty.

Prayer starter: Our Great Father, we wonder why calamity falls upon us. Whatever the reason, help us to know our limitations. Let us be wise enough to see what we have the ability to take care of, and let us give You what is much too huge to tackle.

Jehoshaphat

Part V

God completely and utterly destroyed Jehoshaphat's enemies. A vast and powerful army, one he could never defeat on his own with his own cunning and resources had come against him. There was no hope but in the Lord to save the Kingdom of Judah. And when Jehoshaphat and all of Judah came together to pray for the Lord's rescue, God demolished their enemy and granted peace in the aftermath. *"And the kingdom of Jehoshaphat was at peace, for his God had given him rest on every side"* (2 Chronicles 20:30).

Devotional thought: Jehoshaphat learned about the true meaning of having faith in God. Jehoshaphat learned that it is God who brings peace, not the power of one's abilities. Jehoshaphat watched the Creator bring peace and rest on every side during the most difficult of times.

I hope we learn that no matter what befalls us – sword, famine, calamity, or sickness – the only path is with God the Creator. We are children of the only God. As only a good and loving Father can, He gives us peace and rest when no one else can.

We are not to tremble in rough times. Instead, we are to say, "Here's another one for You, Father. I will step aside and watch in amazement." Trust in God, and peace and rest shall be yours.

Prayer starter: Father, all we can say is thank You. You created us. You are the caregiver. Let us praise You with all our being.

Jesus Endures

Part I

At the beginning of the book of Luke chapter 4, Jesus, full of the Holy Spirit, was led by the Spirit into the wilderness where He was tempted for 40 days and 40 nights. Jesus had just been baptized by his "way maker," John the Baptist. One of Jesus' temptations that is specifically mentioned is recorded in Luke 4:5-7:

> *The devil led him up to a high place and showed him in an instant all the kingdoms of the world. And he said to him, "I will give you all their authority and splendor; it has been given to me, and I can give it to anyone I want to. If you worship me, it will all be yours."*

Devotional thought: I've pondered deeply on this temptation from the wilderness. The scene before us is this: The plan of salvation, which was decided before time, hinges on how Jesus replies. Forty days without food can make a person do things they ordinarily wouldn't do. To say Jesus is physically weak would be an understatement. In this worldly offer that the devil gave Jesus, I wonder if in the seconds before He replied that He paused to consider it. I wonder about the thoughts whirling around in Jesus' mind, that He would be dying for a world that did not recognize Him—that three years down the road, He would be so severely beaten, that His facial features would be unrecognizable; that He would be nailed to hang in public, humiliated, on a Roman cross. Did He think about the crowds chanting, "Crucify Him! Crucify Him!" What about His disciples who will deny Him? Jesus was there when all creation occurred and the plan for salvation was written. He knows all of these things will come to pass and that they will be extremely painful and difficult.

Acceptance of Satan's temptation and Jesus' possession of all the earthly kingdoms was a quick and easy nod away, a barely perceptible motion, and He could skip all the hard parts and come up with the prize. But a prize tainted by the evil of the devil's schemes would make Jesus beholden to him. But thanks be to God, there was nothing more pressing to our Lord Jesus than for Him to carry out the will of His Father in Heaven. Jesus says to Satan in Luke chapter 4 verse 8, *"It is written: 'Worship the Lord your God and serve him only.'"*

Prayer starter: Dear Father, develop in me a heart like Jesus, led by no one but You.

Jesus Endures

Part II

At the beginning of Luke chapter 4, Jesus is led into the wilderness and tempted relentlessly by the devil. Exhausted and starved from fasting, Jesus remains steadfast to His Father's plan, not giving in to the devil's schemes. Yet, at the end of this encounter, Luke foreshadows that there will be at least one other encounter with the devil in verse 13: *"When the devil had finished all this tempting, he left him until an opportune time."*

Devotional thought: The devil failed in his attempt to destroy the plan of salvation to a hungry and exhausted Jesus. But even though the devil left Him, he would return.

The night before Jesus was to be brought before the Pharisees, accused, and crucified, Jesus took His disciples to pray into the Garden of Gethsemane on the Mount of Olives. He knew what was to happen the next day. He knew how it was to happen. He knew the pain He would suffer. And still, He knew He had to fulfill His Father's Will and the plan of salvation for the world. Jesus's most vulnerable time was in the garden. While in the garden, Jesus fully understood the physical torture awaiting Him, but it was Jesus' emotional and mental anguish that the devil would use to try and break the only one who could save us. Mark writes that Jesus was so deeply distressed and troubled that Jesus told His disciples, *"My soul is overwhelmed with sorrow to the point of death"* (Mark: 14:34). In Matthew, Mark, and Luke, Jesus is recorded as asking the Father to find another way if possible. Surely, Satan is in Jesus' ear. It is not recorded, but I wonder if the devil was reminding Jesus that He could have all the Earth's kingdoms if He would just take the easy way out – bow to Satan – because death is not required. Do you really want to die for a world that disowns you?

Luke records that Jesus' sweat was like drops of blood falling to the ground and that an angel came from Heaven to strengthen Jesus. Was the angel strengthening Jesus to prevent His premature death? What if the Savior died from anguish before shedding His blood on the cross?

You see, the devil had so many ways to destroy salvation, but he failed. God's plan never fails. Jesus endured for you and me.

Hallelujah!

Praise His name!

Prayer starter: Thank You, Father! What else can I say?

Jesus our God and Savior

Devotional thought: Some modern-day believers in God (as well as those in the past) have been misinformed about Jesus. Even today, many believe Jesus is a created being, the first creation of God. They say He is the firstborn, a good man, but only a man and that he is not God-made flesh or in human form.

This is false teaching. Even today, Satan has deceived many into believing this. Jesus and God, along with the Holy Spirit, are one. They are eternal: no beginning, no end. God is a Trinity: Father God, Son Jesus, and Holy Spirit. They are three units of a single entity. If an image helps you, picture an apple: the skin, the meat, and the core. Together, they are an apple yet three distinct pieces. By this logic, the Messiah, the Promised Deliverer, has already come into the world in the form of Jesus—God-made flesh.

Friends, no one else is coming to save you. Scripture has been fulfilled. The Messiah, who is God over all, sacrificed His life for you and made you clean by His blood. This fact is illustrated in the writings of the prophet Isaiah in chapter 53 verses 5 and 12. Verse 5: *"But he was pierced for our transgressions, he was crushed for our iniquities... and by his wounds we are healed."* Verse 12: *"For he bore the sin of many, and made intercession for the transgressors."* Other verses that plainly reference Jesus' deity include:

Romans 9:5: *"Theirs are the patriarchs and from them is traced the human ancestry of the Messiah, who is God over all, forever praised! Amen."*

John 1:1: *"In the beginning was the Word, and the Word was with God, and the Word was God." (Here, "the Word" is substituted for "Jesus" as referenced many times throughout Scripture.)*

John 1:14: "The Word became flesh and made his dwelling among us." (Again, "the Word" is a reference to Jesus.)

John 10:38: "Jesus says, 'I and the Father are one.'"

Prayer starter: Father, thank You for dying for us. Give us the wisdom to recognize You, Jesus, as God and Messiah, Savior of all.

John 11

During Jesus's ministry, He had a friend called Lazarus who had taken ill and was close to death. His sister, Mary, had sent messengers to inform Jesus of Lazarus' sickness. Mary asked Jesus to heal Lazarus, for they heard and saw Jesus healing the sick many times before. Jesus delayed on purpose and arrived too late to save Lazarus from the grave as he had been buried four days previously. But Jesus meant to arrive exactly when He did, and He was just in time for what He meant to do and teach the disciples. In John 11:25-26, Jesus replies to Mary's questions about his late arrival and her affirmation that the Lord will grant Jesus whatever He asks: Jesus said to her, *"I am the resurrection and the life. The one who believes in me will live, even though they die; and whoever lives by believing in me will never die. Do you believe this?"*

Devotional thought: Do you believe this? And if you do, does your life reflect Christ? As one of my dear friends has always said, "Is there enough evidence in your life to convict you of being a Christian?"

God has done all He can to offer you salvation. The final sacrifice was made in Jesus at the cross, and God raised Him from the dead. You can believe in the Giver of Life; of that you can be sure!

Purpose is found for those in Christ. If you are looking for purpose in life, look no further than Jesus, for He is the resurrection and the life. It is for Him we should live and dedicate our lives. Everything we do, from the smallest act to the largest, should be to glorify and honor Him. That is our purpose.

Whether you are Christian or not, Christ has the final say on the Last Day concerning who is raised to life and who is doomed eternally. I hope you take time to reflect on your relationship with the Father. I hope you hear Him calling for you, and that you accept His invitation to live your life for Him. I'll end with the words from John 3:16: *"For God so loved the world that he gave his one and only Son, that whoever believes in him shall not perish but have everlasting life."*

Prayer starter: Thank You for revealing Jesus to us—the resurrection and the life. Help us to reflect the life of Jesus every day of our lives. Father, You are awesome!

John 17

In John 17, Jesus is recorded praying to His Father in Heaven for His disciples and then for all believers—those who will come to know Him through the teachings of the disciples. Here, Jesus is looking forward through time and seeing you, here and now, learning and studying His words through the biblical writings.

> Verse 24: *"Father, I want those you have given me to be with me where I am, and to see my glory, the glory you have given me because you loved me before the creation of the world."*

Unfathomable.

Jesus is requesting to the Father that I may enter and see His heavenly dwelling. He wants me with Him! He made a special request!

> Verse 26: *"I have made you known to them, and will continue to make you known in order that the love you have for me may be in them and that I myself may be in them."*

Through Jesus, I know God. God's love has been given to me, and the Spirit of Jesus dwells in my innermost being.

Devotional thought: Jesus revealed Himself to us so that we can know what God is like. The origin of love is God. I love because God loved me first. This is the most fascinating revelation from

God the Creator. And God loves us so much that He wants us to be with Him in His dwelling place forever.

Praise God!

Praise God!

Praise God!

Prayer starter: How can this be, Father? Before creation, You knew I would fail and disappoint you. You give and give, and I sin and sin, but Your love is incomprehensible. You still want me.

Luke 5: 1-11

Jesus wasn't too long into His ministry when Luke tells the following story:

> *Some Jewish fishermen – Peter, Andrew, James, and John – had been fishing all night but didn't catch a thing. The next day, in the same vicinity, a great crowd of people came to Jesus near the shore of the Sea of Galilee to listen to him preach. There was such a large number of people that they pressed in on Jesus, so he asked to get into Peter's boat while preaching to get some space from the crowd. After he had finished speaking, Jesus told Peter to go out a bit deeper and let down the nets to catch some fish. Although Peter was tired from the previous night's fishing, he obeyed Jesus and let down the nets. Luke says the catch was so big that the nets began to tear, and they had to have help hauling in the catch. The astonished Peter came to shore, fell on his knees before Jesus, and exclaimed, "Go away from me, Lord; I am a sinful man!"*

Devotional thought: Peter was overcome by this event. He realized, at that moment, that someone other than an ordinary man was in his presence. He fell to his knees and confessed that he was too great a sinner to be in the presence of the Lord.

I hope you have experienced a moment of awe like that, one that has taken you to your knees at the feet of Jesus. Perhaps you didn't exclaim, "Away from me, Lord, for I am a sinner," but some other indescribable utterance from your innermost being. And if you have not yet been so shaken to your core as to fall to your knees, knowing you are unworthy of the Savior of the World, I hope that moment is not far off for you. For then, Jesus will lift you up and say to you as He did to Peter, *"Don't be afraid, from now on you will fish for people,"* (Luke 5:10), meaning that He will now use you as His disciple to bring others to Him.

Prayer starter: Father, thank You for moments like these when our eyes are fully open to how great You are above all others.

Luke 9:23-26

Part I of IV

Emphasis on Verse 23

In the latter part of Luke chapter 9, Jesus swears His disciples to secrecy then predicts His death, saying that on the third day He will be raised to life. After this profound pronunciation, He tells them other mind-blowing things that would be hard for anyone to digest, starting in verse 23 (through 26):

> *"Then he said to them all: 'Whoever wants to be my disciple must deny themselves and take up their cross daily and follow me. For whoever wants to save their life will lose it, but whoever loses their life for me will save it. What good is it for someone to gain the whole world, and yet lose or forfeit their very self? Whoever is ashamed of me and my words, the Son of Man will be ashamed of them when he comes in his glory and in the glory of the Father and of the holy angels.'"*

Devotional thought: To get a handle on verse 23, it really helps me to examine two things. First, I examine the word "want." Am I sure I "want" to give up my worldly ways for Jesus' ways? Do I "want" to surrender my kingdom for His Kingdom and give up all that I am for all that He is? He is not making you follow Him. He is inviting you to follow Him. Secondly, I think about the question Jesus asked about the man who wanted to build a tower. Jesus asks, *"Won't he first sit down and estimate the cost to see if he has enough money to complete it?"* (Luke 14:28). In other words, why start if you know you can't or won't complete it? It would be time and money wasted.

You see, "taking up your cross daily" means, at times, this new mission you decided to embark upon will be long and burdensome. You have to do it every day. That's the whole point. Many have begun strong, but many have fallen away.

I think of it this way: Jesus, in whom all things were created, and his Father, the God of all, are inviting you to join their team. It will be a rewarding yet sometimes difficult journey. But in the end, it will be grand to hear Jesus say, *"Well done, my good and faithful servant!"* (Matthew 25:21)

Prayer starter: Father, help me to hear Your invitation. Teach me to deny myself and, in everything I do, do it to glorify You every day of my life.

Luke 9:23-26

Part II of IV

Emphasis on Verse 24

After predicting his death in Luke 9, Jesus makes many profound statements that bear further digestion. Focus on what He says in verse 24 in this passage from Luke 9:23-26:

> *"Then he said to them all: 'Whoever wants to be my disciple must deny themselves and take up their cross daily and follow me. For whoever wants to save their life will lose it, but whoever loses their life for me will save it. What good is it for someone to gain the whole world, and yet lose or forfeit their very self? Whoever is ashamed of me and my words, the Son of Man will be ashamed of them when he comes in his glory and in the glory of the Father and of the holy angels.'"*

Devotional thought: To help me understand verse 24, I look at the lives of Judas the betrayer and Paul the apostle—Judas, who cared mostly about his kingdom, and Paul, who gave up all he was.

The book of John says that Judas was in charge of the money. Elsewhere, Judas is said to have helped himself to the treasury. Here's my conclusion on Judas: He is a man so intent on taking care of himself, ignoring the greater good, and rejecting the Author of life that he betrayed Jesus to the authorities, resulting in his final capture and crucifixion. The result is this: He tried to save his life with money and earthly treasure yet lost it when he later took his life out of guilt.

Paul, though, was a man who could boast about his qualifications. He was a Hebrew of Hebrews who could trace his ancestry back to the tribe of Benjamin. In regard to the law, he was a Pharisee of Pharisees because his righteousness based on the law was faultless. But instead of using those qualities for his gain, Paul, after one life-changing moment, surrendered all he was to his Lord and Savior Jesus Christ. In all Paul did, from building tents to speaking with others, he did it to teach others about Jesus. Paul "lost" his previous life and boast-worthy status, but he gained Jesus and saved himself and others.

Prayer starter: Father, we are blind, and our lives are lost without You. Open our eyes to that knowledge, and in Your faithfulness, lead us out of darkness and into our eternal life with You.

Luke 9:23-26

Part III of IV

Emphasis on Verse 25

To further focus on the self-reflective statements Jesus drops on His disciples after predicting His death at the hands of the Pharisees in Luke chapter 9, direct your attention to verse 25, starting in verse 23:

> *"Then he said to them all: 'Whoever wants to be my disciple must deny themselves and take up their cross daily and follow me. For whoever wants to save their life will lose it, but whoever loses their life for me will save it. What good is it for someone to gain the whole world, and yet lose or forfeit their very self? Whoever is ashamed of me and my words, the Son of Man will be ashamed of them when he comes in his glory and in the glory of the Father and of the holy angels.'"*

Devotional thought: Satan is the great deceiver. Satan will use what is temporarily tangible, worldly possessions and status, to camouflage our hope of a reward with the Lord in Heaven which he knows is temporarily invisible. Whether a desire for earthly power, money, fame, or material things, the Christian needs to always be on guard against what is short-lived and meaningless.

I can see, touch, taste, hear, and smell. Many things are pleasing to the senses; therefore, I yearn to accumulate what is of a physical nature. This can be a trap, especially if I find that all my satisfactions and desires are dependent on the visible (Earth) and not the invisible (God). We should strive to reverse this tendency and follow what Paul tells the church at Corinth: *"So we fix our eyes not on what is seen, but on what is unseen, since what is seen is temporary, but what is unseen is eternal."* (2 Corinthians 4:18).

What Luke 9:25 is saying is that if we are overcome by fulfilling ourselves, even if we could gain the whole world, we are actually losing ourselves because we are turning our backs on the only One who can actually give us something meaningful and good. Striving to gain things in this life, as opposed to focusing on God's Heavenly Kingdom, is like settling for a crumb when you could have the whole cake. There is no comparison, and Luke equates it to "losing [your] very self" because you get lost in the pursuit of stuff.

Prayer starter: Heavenly Father, please open my eyes so that my hopes and desires are fixed on the unseen and not on gaining status and possessions in this temporary world. Jesus, focus my heart on You.

Luke 9:23-26

Part IV of IV

Emphasis on Verse 26

The last verse we will focus on in this section of Luke 9 is game-changing. Jesus finishes telling His disciples that He must suffer, be killed, and then raise to life on the third day. Those seem like ridiculous words to this group of His followers. Then, in verse 26, He says not to be ashamed of His words. That is a tall order for the disciples in a time when nothing like this has ever been heard. Luke 9: 23-26 reads:

> *"Then he said to them all: 'Whoever wants to be my disciple must deny themselves and take up their cross daily and follow me. For whoever wants to save their life will lose it, but whoever loses their life for me will save it. What good is it for someone to gain the whole world, and yet lose or forfeit their very self? Whoever is ashamed of me and my words, the Son of Man will be ashamed of them when he comes in his glory and in the glory of the Father and of the holy angels.'"*

Devotional thought: Each person on Earth will hear one of two verdicts from Jesus when He comes in all His glory: 1) *"Well done, my good and faithful servant"* or 2) *"Away from me, I* *never knew you."* We call this the Last Day, the Judgement, the Day of Reckoning. I have no idea when it will come or how it will unfold, but make no mistake that it is coming. On that day, for those who are ready and waiting on His return, those who fully accept Jesus as Lord and Savior, what a glorious ending to life on this Earth—eternity with God. But for those who disown Jesus, who are ashamed of Him and ignore His saving grace, what a dreadful ending to life on this Earth—eternal torment and darkness without mercy.

Paul writes, *"Wake up, sleeper, rise from the dead, and Christ will shine on you"* (Ephesians 5:14). My wife and I are looking forward to that day. We've been washed in the blood of Jesus. We know to whom we belong. God dwells in us now. Our lives have been very blessed yet, at times, extremely hard. But no matter what trials we face on Earth, the peace of Jesus lives in us. I hope it lives in you, too.

Prayer starter: Father, help me to be unashamed in proclaiming Your words so that on the Last Day, I am ready to accept Your glory. And give me the heart to wake the lost, that they, too, may have life in You.

Matthew 8

The Storm

I read an uplifting piece from my Bible's commentary section. The writer reflects on the story of when Jesus calmed the storm on the Sea of Galilee. It reads as follows:

> *Although the disciples had witnessed many miracles, they panicked in this storm. As experienced sailors, they knew its danger; what they did not know was that Christ could control the forces of nature. We often encounter storms in our life where we feel God can't or won't work. When we truly understand who God is, however, we will realize he controls both the storms of nature and the storms of the troubled heart. Jesus' power that calmed this storm can also help us deal with the problems we face. Jesus is willing to help us if only we ask him. We should never discount his power even in terrible trials* (Barker, 2011).

Devotional thought: Like the author of this commentary said, Jesus has the power, not only over the natural storms but the emotional storms as well. He is powerful. He can do all things. He created the Heavens and the Earth. Do you not think He can handle a little rain or emotional turbulence?

When I think of how God is always on my side, I think of Paul's words to the Romans living under Caesar. Even though they were being persecuted by the King of Rome, Paul gives them these words of encouragement: *"If God is for us, who can be against us?"* (Romans 8:31). No storm is too big for God to handle. With God on our side, there is no amount of rain that can flood our spirit. God bless, and peace be upon you.

Prayer starter: Jesus, thank You for calming all life's storms. Help us remember that with You on our side, no storm is too great.

Matthew 11

Jesus proclaims many things about himself throughout recorded Scripture. In Matthew 11:28-30, Jesus says:

> *Come to me, all you who are weary and burdened, and I will give you rest. Take my yoke upon you and learn from me, for I am gentle and humble in heart, and you will find rest for your souls. For my yoke is easy and my burden is light.*

Devotional thought: There is so much bad news in our times. In listening to it, we hear all the troubles of every nation. It's repeated 24 hours a day. I wonder if God is saying stop it!

Let the world's people worry about the world. Let God's people, you and me, come to Jesus with all our burdens and cast all our anxieties upon Him. Try it for one hour, then one day, then one week, and so on. You will experience peace like never before. Today, why not focus on loving one another? Give someone an encouraging word, help a stranger, or give a cool drink of water to someone. Just be grateful for all God's blessings. Jesus will lift your burdens and give you rest. His teachings will give you the ability to love Him and one another without stress or anxiety. And when we love one another, there is peace on Earth.

Prayer starter: Father, please give us Your wisdom in dealing with worldly issues. Remind us not to be burdened with them, but that our mission is to serve You and to love one another as You love us. Let us take rest in You.

My God Is Awesome

"Do you not know? Have you not heard? The Lord is the everlasting God, the Creator of the ends of the earth. He will not grow tired or weary, and his understanding no one can fathom. He gives strength to the weary and increases the power of the weak. Even youths grow tired and weary, and young men stumble and fall; but those whose hope in the Lord will renew their strength. They will soar on wings like eagles; they will run and not grow weary, they will walk and not be faint" (Isaiah 40:28-31).

Devotional thought: Those words from Isaiah display many of God's attributes. Adjectives evident in those verses with which we can describe God include everlasting, creator, persevering, omnipresent, omniscient, omnipotent, rejuvenating, strengthening, trustworthy, and steadfast. Watch out, world! My God is awesome and can do anything. May God bless you each day.

Prayer starter: Everlasting God, You who can do all things, stand by me, and hold me up when I do not have the strength to stand on my own.

My Place of Refuge

Devotional thought: When a deer flees from its attacker, it can escape with a short, quick burst of speed. Many predators relinquish the chase quickly. They are no match for the deer's keen senses and incredible speed. However, when a more powerful enemy gives chase, the advantage is no longer in favor of the deer. The deer's attacker is built for the long run. Distance is the predator's ally. That's its plan—to run the prey to the point of exhaustion and surrender.

Christians may often find themselves in the same predicament as the deer. We may self-extinguish some attacks, but some assaults will lead to exhaustion. As the exhausted and weary deer is no match for the powerful lion, we are no match for the devil who has been perfecting his attack method on mankind since the beginning of time.

So, what shall we do?

How do we escape?

To whom shall we go?

Jesus invites us to the only place of refuge: Himself. Jesus says:

> *Come to me, all you who are weary and burdened, and I will give you rest. Take my yoke upon you and learn from me, for I*

am gentle and humble in heart, and you will find rest for your souls. For my yoke is easy and my burden is light (Matthew 11:28-30).

Jesus goes on later to say, *"Whoever wants to save their life will lose it, but whoever loses their life for me will find it,"* (Matthew 16:25) and *"So the last will be first, and the first will be last"* (Matthew 20:16).

Odd, isn't it?

When we fight, we lose; when we surrender, we are victorious; when we exalt ourselves, God will usually humble us; when we humble ourselves to God, He will always exalt us. God is not interested in your power. He wants you to rely upon His power. You may think you can face the devil alone, but however strong you think you are, the devil can outlast you if you don't rely on God to help you. Lean on Him, and He will get you through the hard times, through the times you feel go on forever. God will lead you on.

Prayer starter: Father, let me know my limitations and that Jesus is always my haven. Help me to come to Him daily. Let my power be only in Him.

Oh, My Soul!

Peter, an apostle of Jesus Christ throughout his ministry on Earth, speaks to the churches in Rome undergoing temptation and persecution: *"Dear friends, I urge you, as foreigners and exiles, to abstain from sinful desires, which wage war against your soul"* (1 Peter 2:11). Those words are just as necessary for us today as they were back then.

Devotional thought: The soul reveals the true person. If one could actually see my soul, it may be appalling to look upon, as it would truly resemble a battlefield. Surveying my soul, I see deep penetrating wounds—some that remain open and oozing solely because of self-choice (stubbornness). Deep scars show evidence of the many battles I have invited by choosing not to abstain from the sinful desires that wage war against me. It's plain to see that flirting with sin will wage a spiritual war within my soul, a perpetual battle I never win.

There are many ways to deny sin the opportunity to wage war: Abstain from sinful desires, do not resurrect the old way of life, and avoid people who lead you to temptation. Keep sin at bay by continually asking the Father for His guidance and strength. Alone, we are no match for Satan, but with God, victory is assured. *"For the wages of sin is death, but the gift of God is eternal life in Christ Jesus our Lord"* (Romans 6:23).

Prayer starter: Father, give us wisdom. Help us plainly see the damage that flirting with sin will cause. Strengthen us that we may abstain from the evil desires we once buried.

Overwhelmed

The early Jewish King David, appointed by God for His righteousness, fell into sin. Beautiful Bathsheba was not his own, but he wanted her so badly that David's lust for her caused him to murder Bathsheba's husband, Uriah (2 Samuel 11). What he did to Uriah was disgusting. He murdered Uriah by sending him into the front lines of a battle with the Ammonites, knowing he would be killed so he could have Bathsheba for his own.

Devotional thought: Sometimes we get into overwhelming predicaments. After the smoke clears and we come to our senses, we realize there is no one to blame but ourselves. Selfishness and jealousy are reasons we get into such horrible situations. We hang our heads in dismay and say, "This can't be happening! What have I done? This is too much!"

Many Christians are deceived. The fall is just a matter of time. No one is perfect. Everyone sins. *"For all have sinned and fall short of the glory of God"* (Romans 3:23). The result of falling into sin brings catastrophe to you and your family. I've seen this firsthand.

So, what now?

You can't dwell in your despair. Your first response should be like David's—recognition of wrongdoing and confession to God:

"I have sinned against the Lord" (2 Samuel 12:13). Later, the prophet Nathan tells David that the Lord has forgiven him.

Prior to your fall, you were full of self-righteousness and jealousy, and bitterness. Your thinking was flawed, and the devil pounced. If you humbly ask, God will forgive you just as He forgave David. You've learned a lesson. You have come to know that the devil prowls like a lion looking for someone to devour. You became his target because of your weakness, and he consumed you. All humans are weak in this way. In time, but only if you allow Him, God can raise you up into a mighty force. He will rebuild you into more than you can imagine, but only if you let Him in, only if you allow the transformation. The choice is yours.

Prayer starter: Heavenly Father, my sins are disgusting. I want to be made new. Give me the wisdom to surrender to You wholeheartedly.

The Parable of the Sower

In Matthew 13, there is a parable Jesus tells in the Bible that demonstrates the impartiality and even-handedness of our God. It shows that the Creator withholds His good news from no one. As a farmer spreads the seed (the Word) in the field, it lands all over, not just falling in a single type of soil. It falls on the hard path that the farmer is walking, the good soil, and everywhere in between. The wise are ready for the Word; it sprouts and takes firm root. The foolish have no time for it; the wind sweeps it away before the first leaf forms.

Devotional thought: God has given His beautiful message to all. Many will never take it to heart, study it, and live it—not because it's difficult but because of a preoccupation with their self-interests. Oh, what tricks Satan plays on the foolish. The seed, the Word, is given, but it is ignored in favor of other things perceived as more important.

Prayer starter: Father, when we speak Your Message to others, let our words be clear. Open the hearts of all who hear Your Word so it may be received and take firm root.

Paul's Prayer

Devotional thought: Paul, in his letter to the church at Ephesus, prays for them. In love for all who are searching for a better and truer way of life, I pray this same prayer for you:

> *... I kneel before the Father, from whom every family in heaven and on earth derives its name. I pray that out of his glorious riches he may strengthen you with power through his Spirit in your inner being, so that Christ may dwell in your hearts through faith. And I pray that you, being rooted and established in love, may have power, together with all the Lord's holy people, to grasp how wide and long and high and deep is the love of Christ, and to know this love that surpasses knowledge – that you may be filled to the measure of all the fullness of God* (Ephesians 3:14-19).

Peace be upon you.

Prayer starter: O Lord, my God, how great thou art. Let me seek Your greatness daily!

Planting

Devotional thought: Suppose I am chosen by my earthly father to become his gardener. He asks that I sow his seed during planting season. In his wisdom, he supplies me with the "Gardening Bible." I diligently study my bible, and it isn't very long before I know its contents cover to cover. Quoting from it flows easily. I also attend countless seminars pertaining to gardening. I become so knowledgeable in this field that experts call on me for advice. Finally, spring arrives. It's getting time to plant. Just to be sure I haven't overlooked something, I re-read the Gardening Bible, word for word, and review all my notes from the uncountable seminars previously attended. I meticulously spray the weeds, till the soil to the exact depth, and apply just the right amount of fertilizer. I think, "Surely, I will reap in abundance when it is time to harvest." Later, I walk in my garden twice a week to check its progress, but surprisingly, I find no growth, not even a weed. I had studied in depth with my fellow gardeners to ensure I had it right. They assured me that my knowledge of gardening was extraordinary, but still, nothing grew. The harvest never came for my earthly father.

I never planted the seed!

Speaking for myself, I can become so sidetracked with "busy" work at church, that I lose focus on the Great Commission:

Go and make disciples of all nations, baptizing them in the name of the Father and of the Son and of the Holy Spirit, and teaching them to obey everything I have commanded you (Matthew 28:19-20).

How many church services and seminars must I attend before I'm ready to plant His Word in someone's heart? I agree knowledge is important, but nothing grows without planting.

Prayer starter: Father, please help me to realize that just "preparing" will never grow Your Kingdom. Help me to put into action all the knowledge You have given me and actually plant Your Word in someone's heart.

Praying for Others

Devotional thought: Many times, we have prayed for a loved one or a friend searching for answers to find God. Sometimes, we wonder if we have said too much or not enough to our friend or loved one. Other times, we want to throw our hands up in frustration at what we see as their lack of progress in finding God.

Think of how Jesus must have felt. He must have become so discouraged at times when dealing with His disciples while on the Earth. On one occasion, when His disciples could not drive out a demon-possessed boy, Jesus said to them, *"How long shall I put up with you, how long shall I stay with you?"* (Mark 9:19). Shortly after, the Lord's disciples argued among themselves about which one of them is the greatest. I reckon Jesus was frustrated. But Jesus kept teaching the disciples until they trusted Him wholeheartedly, until they believed in Him with everything they had, until death. Be patient with those you are mentoring. Keep praying, for God is faithful. Give the Spirit time to do His work. The seed of God's Word that you have planted in them could have sprouted already. You just may not be able to see the effects quite yet. Jesus knows your heart and your desire for them. He will see it through.

Prayer starter: Father, we know You are patient, wanting all to come to repentance. Help us to be patient with those we mentor. Help us so that we never give up, just as You never give up on us.

Prisoner

Devotional thought: There are three types of prisoners: the common prisoner, the spiritual prisoner, and the unknowing prisoner. They all wear chains, but they are not the same.

Common prisoner: A person held in custody, captivity, or forcible restraint. Without a doubt, a person in this setting knows they are a prisoner.

Spiritual prisoner: A prisoner for Christ, full of the Spirit, one whose purpose is to live for the Father, Son, and Holy Spirit, no matter what they do or where they are; a person who has surrendered his own kingdom and exchanged it for God's Kingdom. Without a doubt, a person in this setting knows they are a prisoner.

Unknowing prisoner: A person who thinks they are their own master; one who is in love with the world; one for whom the kingdom of self reigns supreme; one who doesn't comprehend that Satan is his owner. Without a doubt, a person in this setting does not know they are a prisoner, let alone that they are a prisoner of Satan.

The devil is a master charmer. If he were to jump out at me in a red suit with a pitchfork in hand, I would flee with all due haste. But Satan has had an eternity to perfect a more delicate and infinitely more effective method of trapping his prey. To capture most, this is no challenge. For others, he may need to be more patient with and let worldly issues slowly frustrate and weaken the spirit. We must always be vigilant so that we do not become ensnared by the devil's schemes and become an unknowing prisoner.

Prayer starter: Dear Father, we pray for Your wisdom. Give us the courage to inspect our lives and then fortify them with Your Spirit so that we may trade the devil's chains for Your chains.

Prophesy

Old Testament prophesy:

"He was oppressed and afflicted, yet he did not open his mouth; he was led like a lamb to the slaughter, and as a sheep before its shearers is silent, so he did not open his mouth" (Isaiah 53:7).

New Testament fulfillment:

"Then Pilate asked him, 'Don't you hear the testimony they are bringing against you?' But Jesus made no reply, not even to a single charge – to the great amazement of the governor" (Matthew 27:13-14).

Devotional thought: As God was building my faith in Him, He showed me many beautiful things that would help solidify that belief. Such things include a gorgeous morning and breath-taking sunsets, the complexity of the human body, how vast amounts of land can be delivered from drought by a single thunderstorm (my favorite), the seasons, the constant rotation of the Earth, and countless other fortunes. But what solidified my faith was the fulfillment of prophecy. These prophetic writings foretold the coming of Christ, hundreds and even a thousand years before it occurred. They include the telling of the virgin birth of Jesus to the apostles fleeing when Jesus was arrested. It's amazing.

God has given us many ways to believe in Him. Those are only a few of mine.

God made us all different. But whatever is needed from Him to produce faith in you, He will supply. Remember what Jesus said:

> *Ask and it will be given to you; seek and you will find; knock and the door will be opened to you. For everyone who ask receives; the one who seeks finds; and to the one who knocks, the door will be opened* (Matthew 7:7-8).

Prayer starter: God, You are amazing. Thank You for providing solid ground to root my faith.

Psalm 34:3

King David, one of the Hebrew kings appointed by God, wrote many of the Psalms in the Bible. One such Psalm, number 34, says this in verse 3: *"Glorify the Lord with me; let us exalt his name together."*

Devotional thought: Quiet time with the Heavenly Father, being one on one with God and talking intimately with the Creator is powerful. King David had many quiet times with God. But in this verse, he wants others to join with him in a public manner to exalt God.

Feeling God's presence privately is awesome, but feeling it in a community of like-minded believers who love God just the same and are filled with the same joy knowing that He is our Savior is just as awe-inspiring. I hope you glorify the Lord with those around you and let us all exalt His name together.

Prayer starter: Father, please fill me with Your awesome presence while in community with my brothers and sisters during public worship. Let us sing to You with all our hearts.

Psalm 40:5

"Many, Lord my God, are the wonders you have done, the things you planned for us. None can compare with you; were I to speak and tell of your deeds, they would be too many to declare" (Psalm 40:5).

Devotional thought: In Psalm 40:5, King David speaks his praises to God. From a shepherd boy to a king, from protecting flocks of sheep to leading a nation, David recognizes the hand of God in everything. David's life story is extraordinary and shows that nothing is impossible with God.

Like David, I hope you take the time to see the hand of God in your life—what He has done for you, what He has led you out of, and where He wants to lead you from this point forward. Take time to reflect on this. Like David, if you think hard enough, I have a feeling you will find yourself saying, *"Were I to speak and tell of your deeds, they would be too many to declare."*

Prayer starter: Father, how great You are. From the creation of the world to the ascension of Jesus into Heaven, You had me in mind. Give me the wisdom to see Your love in every moment of life.

Psalm 119:9

Devotional thought: The writers of the Psalms address many issues as well as voicing prayers, praise, exclamations of joy, and admissions of sin. In Psalm 119:9, the psalmist addresses one of the most troublesome issues that Christian parents and the church will struggle with: Future generations staying faithful. The writer asks, "How can a young person stay on the path of purity?" Notice the straightforward answer that follows: "By living according to your word."

God has given wildlife a natural sense of wisdom concerning danger—the wisdom of when to hide or when to flee, when to call for help, or when to be silent. God has revealed His wisdom to us through His every word. The God of all that is good has so wisely given His recipe for a path of purity. All we need to do is open our eyes to see it and follow what it says.

Prayer starter: Father, please help us as Your church to faithfully teach the path of purity. Bless the parents of young children with the full measure of Your wisdom.

Psalm 139

Psalm 139 is all about God creating us and knowing us so intimately yet still loving us deeply. The Hebrew King David, the writer of the Psalm, ends it with these two verses: *"Search me, God, and know my heart; test me and know my anxious thoughts. See if there is any offensive way in me, and lead me in the way everlasting"* (Psalm 139:23-24).

Devotional thought: It is no light matter to be examined by God, but King David is asking this very thing. David wanted the most intimate relationship possible with God. The above two verses are the perfect example of surrendering to the Almighty. The Spirit has worked tirelessly to allow you to understand God's love and God's purpose more fully for you, so there must now be a rebellion in your soul that ends with this battle cry: "No more of me, but all of God!"

Prayer starter: Search me, God, and know my heart. Lead me in the way everlasting.

Psalm 86

In Psalm 86, King David says a prayer to God. The prayer is one I encourage you to read in its entirety, for it is applicable today, but we will focus on verse 11 which reads, *"Teach me your way, Lord, that I may rely on your faithfulness; give me an undivided heart, that I may fear your name."*

Devotional thought: King David had many adversaries and numerous other problems. Some of those problems were brought on by his actions. David was aware of his shortcomings, sins, and problems associated with being a king. He realized he desperately needed and desired an intimate relationship with God. He was seeking the deepest possible relationship with God because God is always faithful.

Do we understand the faithfulness of God?

God's faith-ful-ness to us is never broken. He loves us all day long in spite of our faith-less-ness. God's faithfulness to His children will not waver in our dark and desperate times; God is sure to keep His promises to us even when we break our promises to Him and each other.

Before the creation of the world, God knew we would turn and sin against Him, that we would be faithless toward Him before we even knew Him, yet He loved us so much that He created us anyway. Despite the foreknowledge of our sin, God created us, then saved us through the blood of Jesus His Son. Now that is faithfulness!

Prayer starter: Almighty, give us an undivided heart that relies only on You, for You alone are faithful. Let our hearts know You so that we may fear Your majestic name. Every day, please teach me Your ways.

Regard for the Weak

> *Blessed are those who have regard for the weak; the Lord delivers them in times of trouble. The Lord protects and preserves them – they are counted among the blessed in the land – he does not give them over to the desire of their foes* (Psalm 41:1-2).

Devotional thought: In this Psalm, David asks God to deliver him from his enemies. It seemed to David that even his so-called friends whispered against him. In his weakened mental and emotional state, he felt as if he was standing alone. Oh, for a friend who would have regard for the weak!

If you have regard for the weak, thank you. David says that God will deliver you in times of trouble and that the Lord protects and preserves you. You are counted among the blessed. Have regard for the weak and pay no attention to what others may say or do to you in response, for the Lord will be pleased.

Prayer starter: Dear Father, let me be an encouragement for the weak in times of trouble.

Search Me

In Psalm 139, David illustrates just how small we are and how vast God is in comparison. God formed our smallest parts and knows our smallest thoughts. God is big enough to find us anywhere, and His thoughts would outnumber the grains of sand on the Earth. Yet, in the last two verses of Psalm 139, David asks the all-powerful and all-knowing God to do this: *"Search me, God, and know my heart; test me and know my anxious thoughts. See if there is any offensive way in me, and lead me in the way everlasting"* (Psalm 139:23-23).

Devotional thought: This prayer of David will seldom if ever be said by those who exalt themselves and are in love with the world. They foolishly think they are in control of the uncontrollable. They believe in their own wisdom. In reality, they are foolish, and their sight is dim. Destruction and a great fall await them.

No, this prayer to the Father is reserved for the humble in heart, the poor in spirit, and those who hunger and thirst for righteousness—you know, those who have tried it their own way and miserably failed but now rely on God and never self.

If you have the courage to pray the same words as David, you are volunteering to lie on the potter's wheel and let the Master Craftsman have His way. You are allowing God to search your innermost being, destroy all that is offensive to Him, and create in you a brand-new person. He will create in you more peace, more love, and more understanding than you could imagine. All you have to do is let Him in. He will do the rest. *"Blessed are the pure in heart, for they shall see God!"* (Matthew 5:8).

Prayer starter: Father, create in me a clean heart. Lead me in the way everlasting.

Searching for Spiritual Truths

Paul, in his letter to the church at Ephesus, offers a prayer for them. This prayer is appropriate for us today who seek the understanding of God's plan of reconciliation with mankind that was only possible through Jesus. Paul writes the following:

> *... I kneel before the Father, from whom every family in heaven and on earth derives its name. I pray that out of his glorious riches he may strengthen you with power through his Spirit in your inner being, so that Christ may dwell in your hearts through faith. And I pray that you, being rooted and established in love, may have power, together with all the Lord's holy people, to grasp how wide and long and high and deep is the love of Christ, and to know this love that surpasses knowledge – that you may be filled to the measure of all the fullness of God* (Ephesians 3:14-19).

Devotional thought: Paul's prayer for the church in Ephesus is based on the premise that Christ must be of the highest emphasis in their lives. Notice in this prayer, he is adamantly professing that this true intimate understanding of Christ has its origin in the Spirit of God. God is the giver of spiritual gifts, not humans. So, when searching for who Jesus really is, begin with admitting to God (no matter how weak your faith in God might be) that you are frail and poor in spirit and you need spiritual directions from Him to find spiritual truths. He will more than meet your needs.

Prayer starter: O, Lord, my God, how great thou art. Dwell in me that I may understand what Jesus did for me and so that I may be filled with the measure of all the fullness of Your love.

Self-Righteousness

In Luke 18, when Jesus speaks, I have found that verse 9 convicts my heart: *"To some who were confident of their own righteousness and looked down on everybody else, Jesus told this parable: ..."* This is the opening line of the story of the Pharisee and the tax collector recorded in Luke 18:9-14.

Devotional thought: Because of my sinful nature, I sometimes find it necessary to compare myself to others. In these comparisons, I always see myself as more righteous than the other person. One will always blame and accuse others before one blames himself. Self-righteousness will always blind us to the truth concerning our sin. Looking and comparing myself to the horrific sins and godlessness on our planet, it would not be difficult to acquit myself and repeat the prayer spoken by the Pharisee: *"God, I thank you that I am not like other people – robbers, evildoers, adulterers – or even like this tax collector"* (Luke 18:11).

But reasoning like the Pharisee clearly portrays self-righteousness not true righteousness. Jesus makes it perfectly clear in the parable that exalting oneself before God will never bring about God's justification. It can only bring about self-justification, which is useless. Only through the work of the Holy Spirit can I be transformed. It is only through the Holy Spirit that I can be molded and shaped into a humble, grateful, and thankful person, someone who will be exalted by God instead of myself.

Prayer starter: Great God, keep me humble. Never let me take the credit. Instead, give all credit to the Spirit, which works continually in me.

Seven Reasons Not to Worry

Devotional thought: The following is taken from a commentator's notes in one of my Bibles referencing Matthew 6:25-34. The message is noteworthy. I hope your day is filled with assurance from God that He will "handle it."

These are seven reasons not to worry about anything:

1. The same God who created life in you can be trusted with the details in your life.
2. Worrying about the future hampers your efforts for today.
3. Worrying is more harmful than helpful.
4. God does not ignore those who depend on Him.
5. Worrying shows a lack of faith in and understanding of God.
6. Worrying keeps us from the real challenges that God wants us to pursue.
7. Living one day at a time keeps us from being consumed with worry (*Chronological Life Application Study Bible NLT* 2012 p. 1333).

Those seven reasons perfectly summarize the passage from Matthew. There is no point in worrying. I heard a friend say that worrying about something makes you suffer twice—once before it happens and once when it actually happens. And usually, the time you worry about it is much worse than the time it actually happens. So, why worry?

My favorite part of this passage in Matthew 6 is in verse 27 when he says, *"Can any one of you by worrying add a single hour to your life?"* Obviously, the answer is no. Just as obviously, Matthew is trying to convince his audience of the futility of worrying. *"Therefore do not worry about tomorrow, for tomorrow will worry about itself"* (Matthew 6:34).

Prayer starter: Lord, give us the faith to put tomorrow in Your hands and let You take away our worries.

Solomon's Splendor

"The weight of the gold that Solomon received yearly was 666 talents, not including the revenues from merchants and traders and from all the Arabian kings and the governors of the territories" (1 Kings 10:14-15).

Devotional thought: To say that King Solomon was rich would be an understatement. Twenty-five tons of gold on a yearly basis is incomprehensible. The Scripture goes on to say that King Solomon was greater in riches and wisdom than all the other kings of the Earth and that the whole world sought audience with Solomon to hear the wisdom God had put in his heart.

As a young king, Solomon asked God for a discerning heart. God was pleased with Solomon's request and not only gave him more wisdom than any other but gave him immeasurable riches. Later in life, Solomon's heart turned to other gods that were detestable in the sight of the one true God. As a result, God tore most of the kingdom from Solomon's hand.

So, what should you ask of the living God? Wisdom is certainly on my list, yet my most earnest request would be for faithfulness to God until death. Jesus said:

"Because of the increase of wickedness, the love of most will grow cold, but the one who stands firm to the end will be saved" (Matthew 24:12).

Let nothing tear away your complete and utter devotion to the living God while you exist in this body. Stand firm to the end and you will be saved.

Prayer starter: Father, as I live in this body, I cannot think of anything more important than being faithful to You until death. Not only do I ask this for myself and my family, but also for Your precious church that Jesus died for.

Some Say No

Devotional thought: Since existence, humans have said "no" to God. It's not that they don't believe in God, but that they have no time for God. Many have chosen to satisfy their own desires, or you may say, "Gratify the kingdom of self" as opposed to the Kingdom of God. They believe in a god that makes no demands on their life and behavior. They are satisfied with the old, senile version of God who is happy to just watch His children at play.

In reality, God is the opposite. He wants to change your entire thinking and method of action. He wants to rescue you from an evil world, show you His promises, and give you peace. He will take up residence in your heart and call you His very own. However, the real God will not overpower your free will, although He will give you encouragement and hints along the way that He is calling you to take that step toward Him.

God has done all He can to reconcile you to Him. He came to Earth in Jesus and showed you Himself. You will accept the Author of life entirely or by avoidance, rejecting His calling. Those who have heard God's call begin to flee from Satan and the ways of this world. They are easy to recognize. The gratification of the kingdom of self begins to dissipate. They begin to exhibit humbleness and desire reconciliation with God.

God's Spirit will produce other undeniable changes in their innermost being. They too are obvious to recognize. They will begin to demonstrate real love, joy, peace, patience, kindness, goodness, faithfulness, gentleness, and self-control. These are called the "fruit of the Spirit." These new changes are not generated from within but through God. These changes are God-generated.

The one who rejected Him or has no time and desire for the Creator will produce traits of a different kind. They are also obvious to recognize—committing sexual sins (having sex outside of marriage), being morally bad, doing all kinds of shameful things, worshipping false gods, taking part in witchcraft, hating people, causing trouble, being jealous, angry, or selfish, causing people to argue and divide into separate groups, being filled with envy, getting drunk, murdering, lying, gossiping, and acts of homosexuality. Those are called "acts of the flesh."

Many who are followers of Jesus lived the latter life at one time or another. Certainly, I am one. In God's own way, He has called us away from such things and many have come to their senses. By the grace of our God, we saw the pitiful state we were in spiritually, and it terrified our hearts.

Prayer starter: Father, let us be honest with You and ourselves. We know to whom we belong. Give us Your wisdom. Thank You for Your forgiveness.

Surrender

Luke 8:22-25:

One day Jesus said to his disciples, "Let us go over to the other side of the lake." So they got into a boat and set out. As they sailed, he [Jesus] fell asleep. A squall came down on the lake, so that the boat was being swamped, and they were in great danger. The disciples went and woke him, saying, "Master, Master, we're going to drown!" He got up and rebuked the wind and the raging waters; the storm subsided, and all was calm. "Where is your faith?" he asked his disciples. In fear and amazement they asked one another, "Who is this? He commands even the winds and the water, and they obey him."

Devotional thought: I find it interesting that Jesus had His disciples get in the boat in the first place. Did Jesus not know a storm was approaching? Of course, He did. The disciples had no idea, but Jesus was going to give them a lesson about who controls all things and the Author of peace. When the student (disciple) least expects it, the Master gives instruction.

I have much in common with the disciples regarding panic during my trials and storms. When the water is calm (there are no problems), I foolishly think I am the master at sea. However, under trial, I am the first to scream, "Master, Master, I'm going to drown!"

The disciples had four options during the storm:

1. Jump ship and try in vain to swim to shore which would have meant leaving Jesus (certain death)
2. Fight in vain to empty the boat full of water (ineffective and useless)
3. In an extreme panic, wake Jesus and scream, “Master, can’t you see what’s happening here?” (Basically, what they did.)
4. Come to terms with the fact that the storm is bigger than them, saying, “I can’t predict its outcome. I simply can’t control it. Jesus is aware of its size and won’t let me drown.”

I have found myself in all four categories:

1. Jumping ship, trying to escape the inescapable
2. Futilely attempting to empty the boat of the water
3. Screaming at Jesus
4. Giving up to Jesus what I can’t control.

God has a desire to increase my faith so I can live in this world of uncertainty. My Creator knows when my storms are approaching. Looking back, I can clearly see that I should have examined my options early in all crises and without a doubt should have chosen number four. Any alternative always proves worthless and creates stress beyond measure. Choosing to surrender to God is admitting

I am powerless, but God is able. The act of surrendering is faith in its purest form.

Later, there will be other storms, maybe bigger storms. That's life. There will be times when Jesus takes me again to the other side of the lake to introduce me to my next trial. On such a journey, there will be life-changing experiences and chances for real spiritual growth. When those new trials emerge, I hope I surrender to Jesus' power in the face of all things and put my faith in Him.

Prayer starter: Dear Father, continue to make me aware of how powerless I am in the trials of life so that Your power may be seen. Even when I don't understand, show me how to rely only on You.

Symptoms of Sin

Devotional thought: When the COVID epidemic began, I looked on the CDC website. I was looking for symptoms of the Coronavirus. It stated: "the most common symptoms are fever, tiredness, and dry cough. Most people (about 80%) recover from the disease without needing special treatment." (Coronavirus Disease 2019 (COVID-19)).

Hmm, but what about the deadliest of all diseases—sin?

I looked in the Bible and found that it actually lists a few symptoms of this deadly disease: sexual immorality, impurity, excessive indulgences in sensual pleasures, idolatry, witchcraft, hatred, discord, jealousy, fits of rage, selfish ambitions, envy, drunkenness, telling lies, lust, greed, stealing, unwholesome talk, and adultery. You get the picture. According to that list, you should be able to tell if you have a "sin" infection. Some don't realize that they exhibit any of those symptoms. They go about their lives infecting others without knowing it.

The CDC advises that about 80% of people will recover from the Coronavirus without any help. But what about the sin infection? From the beginning of time, 100% of the human population has been infected with sin with a 0% recovery rate without any help. No one overcomes this disease on their own, and the final outcome is a horrific eternal death. The only remedy is Jesus. Only He can save you.

Have you come to Him?

Can you hear Him calling?

Prayer starter: Dear Father, make us aware of how sick we are without Jesus. Please open our eyes so we may see the Remedy.

Thank You, Father!

Devotional thought: Each morning as we arise, as our five senses slowly awaken and we begin another day, let us be thankful. For if we soberly and truthfully look back on our lives, they are filled with innumerable blessings we cannot begin to fathom. God is great.

Go and tell others of how God has healed you, how He has brought you through your deepest valleys. Share. Give others hope. Do not be silent, but lift God up to others. Tell of His greatness.

Prayer starter: Father, thank You for saving us. Thank You for all Your blessings. Help me to be courageous and tell others of Your splendor.

The Accuser Falls

Job 1:8-11:

> *Then the Lord said to Satan, "Have you considered my servant Job? There is no one on earth like him; he is blameless and upright, a man who fears God and shuns evil." "Does Job fear God for nothing?" Satan replied. "Have you not put a hedge around him and his household and everything he has? You have blessed the work of his hands, so that his flocks and herds are spread throughout the land. But now stretch out your hand and strike everything he has, and he will surely curse you to your face."*

Devotional thought: Have you ever thought of Satan standing before God, accusing us of being disobedient? At some point, Satan (the accuser) had his time in the presence of God. He made accusations against Job and Joshua the High Priest (Zechariah 3). What shall I do when Satan accuses me? Am I a slave to sin, or have I been set free from sin's bondage?

God already knew the answers to those accusations before the creation of the world. Paul writes in Ephesians, *"For he chose us in him before the creation of the world to be holy and blameless in his sight"* (Ephesians 1:4). God knew we would be sinners, but He made a way for us to bc pure again. He gave us Jesus, who gave up Himself for us.

When the time was right, God sent Christ to atone for sin. Christ Jesus endured the cruelties of people and the temptations of Satan yet remained sinless. In Revelation 12:10, John wrote of hearing a loud voice in heaven, saying: "*...For the accuser of our brothers and sisters, who accuses them before our God day and night, has been hurled down. They triumphed over him by the blood of the lamb and by the word of their testimony...*"

Jesus is the lamb without blemish, the perfect sacrifice. Jesus' pure sacrifice defeated Satan once and for all by conquering sin and nailing it to the cross. Now, our crucified but risen Savior is at the right hand of God. Jesus paid the required cost and, as the apostle Paul said to the church in Rome: *"If God is for us, who can be against us?... Who will bring any charge against those whom God has chosen?... Christ Jesus...is at the right of God interceding for us"* (Romans 8:31, 33, 34).

Now, I suppose that the only way for Satan's accusations to have any validity is for one to refuse to be set free, for one to reject the gift of Jesus' pure sacrifice that washes away all our own blemishes.

Prayer starter: Sovereign God, Your wisdom is beyond human understanding. Through the Anointed One, sin has no hold on Your people. Open the eyes of the captives that they may be freed from Satan's accusations. Help them to gratefully receive Your gift. You have opened wide the gates of freedom.

The Day of the Lord

The apostle Peter, speaking about the last days, writes:

> *But the day of the Lord will come like a thief. The heavens will disappear with a roar; the elements will be destroyed by fire, and the earth and everything done in it will be laid bare. Since everything will be destroyed in this way, what kind of people ought you to be?* (2 Peter 3:10-11)

Peter goes on to say in verse 14, *"So then, dear friends, since you are looking forward to this, make every effort to be found spotless, blameless and at peace with him."*

Devotional thought: How are we to be found spotless, blameless, and at peace with God? Let me answer this bluntly: it has nothing to do with you. For if we could be good enough to save ourselves with human effort, then Jesus died for nothing. We know what the Bible says about human effort: *"For all have sinned and have fall short of the glory of God"* (Romans 3:23). What I'm saying is that without the blood of Jesus, all is lost. You can't save yourself. God saves you through Jesus. *"Whoever has the Son has life; whoever does not have the Son of God does not have life"* (1 John 5:12).

Accept the Son. Live!

Prayer starter: Dear Father, please help us to understand that humans cannot be saved by our efforts alone. We are stained in sin without Jesus' sacrifice. Help us, Father, to understand that only You can save us and to accept Your gift of life.

The Illusion

Jesus warns his followers that *"In this world, we will have trouble"* (John 16:33). Jesus also states that your enemy, Satan, is the prince of this world (John 14:30).

Devotional thought: One of the greatest illusions in this world is that everything in our lives should be good. Our troubles should be kept in check, and everything should go our way as we live our earthly lives. In reality, evil and disappointment abound, leaving many in disarray, feeling hopeless, having questions without answers, and living without peace.

So, who can help us find peace as we travel this world? Friends and family? Most definitely, but sometimes, friends and family efforts fall short. Their comfort is not strong enough nor enduring, not because they don't try, but because they cannot see into our souls, the place where we store our deepest feelings and thoughts. If only there was someone who could see into my soul. If only there was someone to whom I could express my deepest feelings and thoughts. Well, the Bible tells us that someone exists. Read carefully what Paul says concerning the Holy Spirit interceding for us: *"In the same way, the Spirit helps us in our weakness. We do not know what we ought to pray for, but the Spirit himself intercedes for us through wordless groans..."* (Romans 8:27). The Holy Spirit sees what is in our hearts and then expresses what we don't know how to say to the Father God through Jesus the Son. They hear you and know you.

Our search for peace must go beyond human flesh and its wisdom. Our search must include our Creator, the Master Potter, the One who made us from the very dust of the Earth, the One who formed us in our mother's womb. Let Him see your heart's thoughts. I hope it helps to know that someone who can truly give you peace is listening.

Prayer starter: Father, I need to trust You more. True peace can only be found in You. Give me the courage to surrender my innermost being into Your hands.

The Parable of the Growing Seed

Part I of II

Trying to explain what the Kingdom of God is like, Jesus used multiple parables to illustrate it. One such story is recorded in Mark 4:26-29: Jesus says:

> *This is what the kingdom of God is like. A man scatters seed on the ground. Night and day, whether he sleeps or gets up, the seed sprouts and grows, though he does not know how. All by itself the soil produces grain – first the stalk, then the head, then the full kernel in the head. As soon as the grain is ripe, he puts the sickle to it, because the harvest has come.*

Devotional thought: From my front porch, I look out at the fields around my house, and I see that the farmers have planted; the fields are jam-packed with crops. Had the farmers not planted, these fields would not be filled with crops but infested with weeds.

In this parable in Mark, I believe Jesus wants us to see two details connected to this story. First, the Father wants me to plant, to be a farmer.

But how?

Through kindness, by encouraging, by caring for someone, by telling someone you're praying for them, and by many other ways through which the Spirit has enabled you. Be a farmer of God's Word. Sow the seed.

Secondly, sit back and watch the Spirit do His work. In John 3, a Pharisee named Nicodemus spoke to Jesus at night. Jesus tells Nicodemus that a man must be born again to become a part of the Kingdom of Heaven. A man cannot enter the Kingdom of God unless he is born again, from above, by the power of the Spirit. Jesus equates the Spirit to the wind in John 3:8, saying, *"The wind goes where it pleases. You hear its sound, but you cannot tell where it comes from or where it is going. So it is with everyone born of the Spirit."* Therefore, let the Spirit do Its work. The Spirit is powerful and does not need any help from me to grow or flourish the seed.

Prayer starter: Dear Father, so many things are mysterious to me. I've witnessed the vilest offenders become Your servants. Only through the power of Your Holy Spirit can an evil man become Your child. Make me a better farmer, then help me sit back and watch the harvest grow in Your Spirit.

The Parable of the Growing Seed

Part II of II

While it could not have been an easy task to try to explain eternity to humanity that can hardly grasp today, Jesus tried his best in the parable of the growing seed as recorded by Mark. In this story, Jesus says:

> *This is what the kingdom of God is like. A man scatters seed on the ground. Night and day, whether he sleeps or gets up, the seed sprouts and grows, though he does not know how. All by itself the soil produces grain – first the stalk, then the head, then the full kernel in the head. As soon as the grain is ripe, he puts the sickle to it, because the harvest has come* (Mark 4:26-29).

Devotional thought: One of the most disappointing things about being a farmer is to have the crop destroyed right before the harvest. The grain is ripe, but then high winds come up that lay the stalks to waste, or a flood rises that prevents the farmer from gathering the grain. The harvest is lost. That's not only true of crops but of seeds planted in the Spirit through the Word of God.

From a seed that was planted by you or someone else, the Spirit then works in an individual to the point where they are ready to give their life to the Creator. Who shall harvest? Jesus tells His disciples, *"The harvest is plentiful but the workers are few. Ask the Lord of the harvest, therefore, to send out workers into his harvest field"* (Matthew 9:38).

Without the worker there is no harvest; the harvest is lost. It rots in the field. How terrible to allow the mature crop to be wasted? How terrible for the Christian to let a brother or sister in Christ do the same? Christians are the workers. They need to step up, be bold, and reap the harvest of those who have been planted in the Spirit. They cannot let fear keep them from bringing others in from the field.

Prayer starter: Heavenly Father, we have no defense before You when we knowingly allow an individual to be passed by. Father, renew my spirit and open my eyes and heart that I may recognize when the harvest is ripe.

The Pull

Paul speaks these chilling words to the church in Corinth: *"Do you not know that wrongdoers will not inherit the kingdom of God?"* (1 Corinthians 6:9).

Devotional thought: What would it take for you to sell out? What earthly pleasures are causing you to waiver in your commitment to Jesus Christ? Sexual immorality, homosexuality, greed, adultery, and hate are just a few of the enticements before you daily. The pull to abandon your faith is massive. The pull never ends. Temptation is so strong that at times you can't reason or think straight; common sense and rational thought have vanished.

James says that when tempted, we are dragged away by our own evil desires (James 1:14). We become so head-strong and blinded by these desires that we are helpless in trying to escape the enticement. How many times can we go down that road? How many times can we make up excuses for the sins we commit? How many times can we say, "This is the last time"?

Paul says that those who continue in sin will not enter the Kingdom of God. I hope that scares you. I hope it makes you extremely uncomfortable to think that you could reject salvation because you prefer to obey your own will rather than God's.

Yes, church folks are Satan's perpetual target. Satan knows they are in a constant war with their evil desires, and he tries to wear them down. I urge you to stay strong and resist the devil.

Prayer starter: Father, may Your Holy Spirit work in me tirelessly. Create in me a new heart.

The Strong Man

Recorded in Luke 11:14-23, you will see that the jealous teachers of religious law question Jesus. They demand to know from whom and where He gets His power to drive out demons. They even accuse Jesus of getting is power from Satan. Jesus answers them in His own fashion, saying, *"A house divided against itself will fall"* (verse 17), meaning that Satan would not drive out his own demons.

In addition to this theme, I see something else in this story, illustrated by verses 21-22:

> *When a strong man, fully armed, guards his own house, his possessions are safe. But when someone stronger attacks and overpowers him, he takes away the armor in which the man trusted and divides up his plunder.*

Devotional thought: Before Jesus' time on Earth, the world was in disorder. Even though the Jews had the Law of Moses, they could not manage to obey it. They are lawbreakers. Instead of the Law saving them, it makes them conscious of their terrible misconduct before the living God.

Well, the non-Jews haven't got a chance. Their gods are made of sticks and stones. Satan is the prince of the world, "the strong man" in the scriptural reference, where humans live out their years. Satan is trying to guard his house against Jesus, for reconciliation with the Creator has yet to occur. But at the right time, Jesus reveals Himself. Immanuel (*"God with us"*), overpowers the strong man and redeems for God what Satan possessed briefly: the human race. The former strong man is defeated forever by One more powerful than he: Jesus.

And now, we wait. We wait upon God to bring this old world in which we live to its finality. We await the new. *"See, I am doing a new thing!"* (Isaiah 43:19).

Prayer starter: Our God, thank You for Your plan of salvation even before time began. Peace and reconciliation are now possible in Jesus Christ.

The Widow from Nain

Luke 7:11-17

"They were all filled with awe and praised God, ... they said, 'God has come to help his people'" (Luke 7:16).

Devotional thought: The widow from Nain—what an incredible story. Luke tells of two crowds converging toward one another and the miracle at their meeting. One crowd is following the miracle worker named Jesus from Nazareth. They are going to a village called Nain. This crowd, full of joy and awe, has seen things that few on Earth have witnessed: the casting out of Satan's demons from human flesh, miraculous healings of incurable diseases, and the gift of sight to the blind.

The other crowd, a funeral procession, is leaving the village of Nain and proceeding to a burial ground. A widow's only son had just died. This widow, and the crowd with her, had just witnessed what they believed to be the finality of life—a hopeless death. This widow, now on her own, has no one to care for her. What good could come from this bleak and miserable day?

As the two crowds merge, Jesus saw this widow and His heart overflowed with compassion. He tells the widow, "Don't cry." At this very moment, the two crowds are closely watching Jesus—one full of joyful anticipation awaiting what this miracle worker might do, and the other thinking how foolish it is to tell this childless widow not to cry.

Jesus approaches the coffin, places His hand upon it, and says to the young man, “Get up!” What happened next brought great fear and awe among the crowd. The dead young man sat up and began to talk. The crowd exclaimed, “God has come to help his people!”

God sees your hour of need, and, as that story illustrates, His heart goes out to you. Do not be downhearted, for God will lift you up.

Prayer starter: What can I say, Father? In the midst of hopelessness, You give hope. Even in death, You give life. How great thou art!

The Wind

"The wind blows wherever it wants. Just as you can hear the wind but can't tell where it comes from or where it is going, so you can't explain how people are born of the Spirit" (John 3:8).

Devotional thought: The above verse is another perplexing verse for me. For as long as I can remember, I've been taught that one receives the Holy Spirit upon baptism. I believe that. Peter says this much in Acts 2:38. But what is the root cause of desiring a relationship with God? Does this desire come from within? Do I, from the flesh, give birth to the Spirit?

No, this is an impossibility because flesh cannot give birth to Spirit. So, I find myself responding the same way Nicodemus did: *"How are these things possible?"* (John 3:9).

If the flesh was the spark for generating a relationship with the Creator, Satan would have no problem with extinguishing such a flame. The weakness of the flesh is no match for him. So, I must think again about what Jesus is saying. Somehow, someway, just as the wind blows, the Spirit touches us. Spiritual conception begins with the Spirit. The Spirit is the catalyst. The Spirit initiates the beginning of our journey to a relationship with God. Along the way, God drops huge hints like the magnificence of nature, influential people, the Word, and comfort in prayer to draw us to Him. We do not seek Him as much as He seeks us! What a great thought to know that the Father is actively seeking each and every one of us and urging us to come to Him. You are special to Him.

Prayer starter: Heavenly Father, thank You for calling us. Thank You that we hear Your call.

Tree of Life

Devotional thought: When trees are well taken care of, watered regularly, and pruned, they reflect God's design for them. They provide beauty, shade, and healthy branches. They even provide homes for various types of wildlife. These healthy branches will sway in fierce winds and withstand prolonged drought. But when a limb becomes damaged and mostly detached from the trunk, it won't be long before it begins to show distress. Leaves fall, and branches begin to partially break. They barely hang on.

Humans can take a lesson from nature—remove the food source, and there is a slow death. When the Christian breaks away from the Son (Jesus), spiritual death may be slow, but it is inevitable. It happens in small ways that we don't recognize, just one fallen leaf. Soon, the whole limb dies and crashes to the ground.

Be on guard. Look for weak and splintered branches in the fellowship of God's people, in your children, and in your loved ones before they completely detach from the trunk.

Prayer starter: Father, we know the schemes of the devil are endless. Help us to notice and act before a loved one detaches from the tree of life.

True and False Disciples

Matthew 7:21-23:

> *Not everyone who says to me, "Lord, Lord," will enter the kingdom of heaven, but only the one who does the will of my Father who is in heaven. Many will say to me on that day, "Lord, Lord, did we not prophesy in your name and in your name drive out demons and in your name perform many miracles?" Then I will tell them plainly, "I never knew you. Away from me, you evil doers!"*

Devotional thought: The above passage is part of the sermon on the mountainside. At the end of Jesus' teaching, Matthew says, *"The crowds were amazed at his teaching because, he taught as one who had authority, and not as their teachers of the law"* (Matthew 7:28-29).

Many teachers of the law, the elders, and the Pharisees who were in high positions exalted themselves instead of the Creator. Even though they were mere humans, they boasted, desired, and demanded recognition. Having the heart to serve and lead the masses of Israelites with love and mercy was not in their interest. Many taught the Scripture only to make a show of themselves. Later, Jesus compares them to "whitewashed tombs." In other words, they looked righteous on the outside, but inwardly, they were rotten. They grandstanded.

Understand what Paul says to the church at Corinth: *"If I give all I possess to the poor and give over my body to hardship that I may boast, but do not have love, I gain nothing"* (1 Corinthians 13:3). If I do good things just so I may boast, I urgently need to re-examine my motive. If self-gratification is my intention, I've missed the entire meaning and concept of God's love. If I serve others for my glory and not God's, it is done in vain, for I gain nothing.

Prayer starter: Father, destroy my self-righteousness. Help me so that my motives are true.

Verses to Ponder

Genesis 1:1 – *"In the beginning God created the heavens and the earth."*

John 1:1-3 – *"In the beginning was the Word, and the Word was with God, and the Word was God. He was with God in the beginning. Through him all things were made; without him nothing was made that has been made."*

John 1:14 – *"The Word became flesh and made his dwelling among us."*

John 1:10-11 – *"He was in the world, and though the world was made through him, the world did not recognize him. He came to that which was his own, but his own did not receive him."*

John 1:18 – *"No one has ever seen God, but the one and only Son, who is himself God and is in closest relationship with the Father, has made him known."*

John 3:16 – *"For God so loved the world that he gave his one and only Son, that whoever believes in him shall not perish but have eternal life."*

Romans 5:6 – *"You see, at just the right time, when we were still powerless, Christ died for the ungodly."*

Romans 3:23-25 – *"For all have sinned and fall short of the glory of God, and all are justified freely by his grace through the redemption that came by Christ Jesus. God presented Christ as a sacrifice of atonement, through the shedding of his blood – to be received by faith."*

Acts 2:24 – *"God raised him from the dead, freeing him from the agony of death, because it was impossible for death to keep its hold on him."*

Acts 2:38-39 – *"Repent and be baptized, every one of you, in the name of Jesus Christ for the forgiveness of your sins. And you will receive the gift of the Holy Spirit. The promise is for you and your children and for all who are far off – for all whom the Lord our God will call."*

Devotional thought: God had this plan of salvation laid out from the beginning. Before man was a grain of sand upon the Earth, God had a plan to send His Son to Earth to make the Father known, then to sacrifice that Son for the sins of the world. Death could not hold the Son, and the Father raised Him on the third day. If we, sinful man, repent of those sins and be baptized into Him, we will receive the Holy Spirit, God's helper and advocate on Earth, to help us. That was the plan. We must only believe, for who are we to think we could know the mind of God or the purpose of the universe?

Prayer starter: Heavenly Father, You are beyond describing! Thank You for Your plan.

Weeping and Gnashing

Matthew 13:41-42:

> *The Son of Man will send out his angels, and they will weed out of his kingdom everything that causes sin and all who do evil. They will throw them into the blazing furnace, where there will be weeping and gnashing of teeth.*

Devotional thought: Not to be too depressing or negative, but we must pay close attention to the warnings which Jesus declares. I say this because many have and will continue to ignore the Son of God even as He pleads for the multitudes to come to their senses. Jesus describes the horrific reaction of those who will eternally depart from Him and the Father: *"Weeping and gnashing of teeth."*

The lost will weep. They will weep to be with the Father, weep while asking for forgiveness, weep as faithful loved ones depart to be with God, weep because they ignored countless warnings to repent, and weep because their eternal home is with the devil and his demons.

The lost will gnash their teeth. They will gnash their teeth as they are tossed into the lake of fire as they realize all hope is gone, a hope which will never return. There is no appeal. There is no second chance. His judgment is real—the finality of this age, the bottom line, and the last word. While it is still today, heed His warning. Hear His call. Do not let your life end without knowing the Father. While it is today, give good direction to those on the wrong path, offer hope to the hopeless, and be merciful to those who doubt.

Prayer starter: Our Father, thank You for Your patience with me. I pray for the lost that they may see Your face before it is too late.

What Is in a Man?

For God so loved the world that he gave his one and only Son, that whoever believes in him shall not perish but have eternal life. For God did not send his Son into the world to condemn the world, but to save the world through him (John 3:16-17).

Devotional thought: What is in a man? What is in a man when, after the Spirit has revealed to him the Creator and Savior, he knowingly ignores this revelation and allows himself and his family to fall away? Jesus warns us of this very thing. Jesus says that this type of person's relationship with the Father is choked out by the cares, riches, and pleasures of life.

What is in a man? The world. It deceives us into forgetting or rejecting our faith in God. Remember what Jesus said, *"For what does it profit a man to gain the whole world and forfeit his soul?"* (Mark 8:36). If we let the world encroach into our souls, it will consume us. Focus instead on the Lord, and He will save you.

Prayer starter: Dear Father, do what You must to open our hearts that we may live for You.

Closing Remarks

In John 16:33, Jesus says, *"I have told you these things, so that in me you may have peace. In this world you will have trouble. But take heart! I have overcome the world."*

Devotional thought: I believe Jesus is saying, "The Earth is not a place where you want to spend eternity—troubles abound. I offer something better. It is perfect and eternal."

As you know, life on Earth is unpredictable. Divorce, illness, suffering, loss of job, depression, accidents, and death will show their ugly faces without warning.

There are several ways we can help ourselves: having good friends to share our troubles with, finding a good therapist, and researching positive ways to deal with these issues. But my first choice would be this: Surrender. Surrender to the Creator of all things. In fact, almost every devotional in this book has this suggestion.

I'll end with the very words of Jesus. They are recorded in the New Testament book of Matthew in chapter 11, beginning in verses 28 through 30:

Come to me, all you who are weary and burdened, and I will give you rest. Take my yoke upon you and learn from me, for I am gentle and humble in heart, and you will find rest for your souls. For my yoke is easy and my burden is light.

Peace to you.

Prayer starter: Dear Father, I know You will see me through this life on Earth. May Your peace abound in me forever. Praise to You, the Father, the Son, and the Holy Spirit.

Epilogue: One Lost Sheep

Luke 15:4-7:

> *Suppose one of you has a hundred sheep and loses one of them. Doesn't he leave the ninety-nine in the open country and go after the lost sheep until he finds it? And when he finds it, he joyfully puts it on his shoulders and goes home. Then he calls his friends and neighbors together and says, "Rejoice with me; I have found my lost sheep." I tell you that in the same way there will be more rejoicing in heaven over one sinner who repents than over ninety-nine righteous persons who do not need to repent.*

I entitled this collection of devotionals "One Lost Sheep" to reference this parable from Luke chapter 15. This parable has always been one of my favorites because it illustrates just how important each and every one of us is to God, the Great Shepherd, even those who wander off and are hopelessly lost in the wilderness. I did not intend to write a 100th devotional, but I came to realize that this final thought was important enough to include in the epilogue.

Devotional thought: In this parable, the shepherd realizes that one of his sheep has gone missing. In the grand scheme of things, one out of 100 is not that devastating. He could have lived comfortably in the knowledge that he had saved the vast majority of his sheep and gone on knowing he had done well. Most shepherds would have done that, but not my Lord. He wants all the sheep to come home, and He will not settle for less. He knows that the ones that have stayed close are safe, so He ventures out to find the lost one. In the story, a journey like this could be risky. There are wolves and lions and all sorts of dangerous predators. There are also canyons, mountains, cliffs, rain, wind, and snow. Any number of perilous obstacles could stand in the path between the shepherd and his sheep, many of them fatal. But my Lord, my Shepherd, pursues the lost anyway.

Jesus stood the test of the Ultimate Shepherd. He sought after a world of lost sinners, fighting through obstacle after obstacle then finally giving up His life to save the lost sheep. He brought us back into the fold by His sacrifice, and now all the angels in Heaven rejoice at each and every sinner, each and every sheep, who repents and accepts the love of Jesus. Jesus is seeking us all, all of us who wander. When we repent, when we vow to live for Him, we are being found and there is much rejoicing in Heaven.

Prayer starter: Jesus, thank You for being the Ultimate Shepherd. Thank You for finding me even when I didn't know I was lost. Please help me to go out and find others of Your flock who are lost as well.

Citations

Barker, K. L. (2011). *The NIV Study Bible: New International Version*. Zondervan.

Barkley, R. (2013). *Looking for God* (Vol. 1 & 2). Doulos Publishing House.

Centers for Disease Control and Prevention. (n.d.). *Coronavirus Disease 2019 (COVID-19)*. Centers for Disease Control and Prevention. Retrieved April 13, 2020, from https://www.cdc.gov/coronavirus/2019-ncov/index.html.

Tyndale House Publishers, Inc. (2012). Seven Reasons Not to Worry. In *Chronological Life Application Study Bible NLT* (2nd ed., p. 1333). essay.

A Special Note

If you suffer from depression, get help now. Do not suffer. Do not suffer by yourself. No matter what it takes, seek help.

My highest degree of learning is a high school education. I have no formal training in the medical field concerning depression. I do, however, have years of firsthand experience with this deadly disease. Because of this, I have a strong desire to assist others the best I can to make sense out of confusion. You may contact me at wbslkt@gmail.com. I promise to do my best to lead you in the right direction.

Made in the USA
Middletown, DE
08 November 2023

42049541R00106